# The book of
# Fortune Telling

# The book of
# Fortune Telling

## The art of divination and clairvoyance

Michael Johnstone

This edition published in 2018 by Arcturus Publishing Limited
26/27 Bickels Yard, 151–153 Bermondsey Street,
London SE1 3HA

AD006193UK

Printed in the UK

# Contents

Introduction ....................................................7

It's on the cards .........................................31

It's in your cups........................................77

It's in the crystal...................................111

It's in the East .........................................121

The I Ching .............................................163

It's in the numbers...............................187

It's in the palm of your hand ............201

It's in the stones....................................229

It's in the stars .......................................249

# Introduction

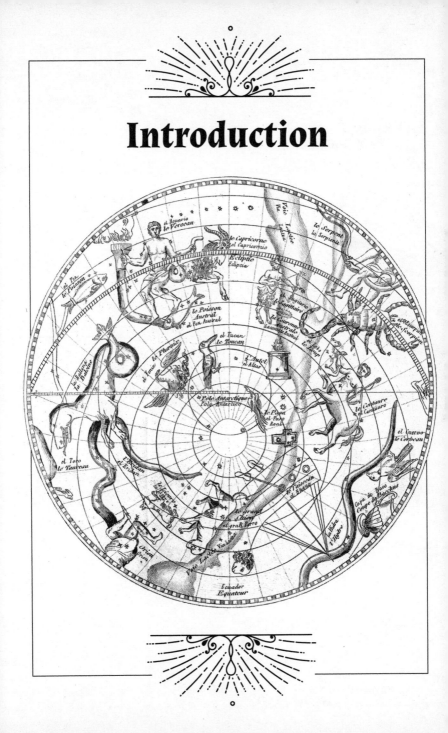

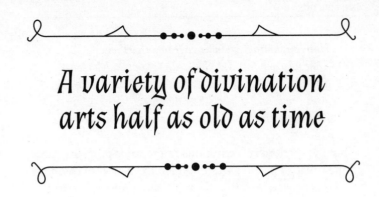

# A variety of divination arts half as old as time

Divination: ME [-()Fr. *divination* or L. *divinatio*, f. *divinat-*, pa, ppl stem of *divinare*; see DIVINE v., -ION.]

1.  The action or practice of divining; the foretelling of future events or discovery of what is hidden or obscure by supernatural or magical means. Also with a [article] and pl. [plural] an exercise of this, a prophecy, an augury.

2.  Successful conjecture or guessing.

Not content with telling us that the word 'divination' is a Middle English one that has its roots in Old French or Latin, and then defining the word, the 1983 edition of the Oxford English Dictionary goes on to tell us that the first recorded written use of the word in its longer meaning is found in the work of Sir Thomas North (c. 1535–c. 1601). The Tudor poet wrote, 'The flying of birds, which doe geue a happy divination of things to come.' The second meaning was first used in written form by North's contemporary, William Shakespeare, who in *Henry IV Part II* wrote:

> '*Why, he is dead.*
> *See what a ready tongue suspicion hath!*
> *He that but fears the thing he would not know*

*Hath by instinct knowledge from others' eyes*
*That what he fear'd is chanced. Yet speak, Morton;*
*Tell thou an earl his divination lies,*
*And I will take it as a sweet disgrace*
*And make thee rich for doing me such wrong.'*

What the dictionary definitions fail to do is give any hint of the breadth of the ways in which the action of divining can be practised. For that we must move several centuries on from Thomas North and William Shakespeare and turn to twenty-first century technology – the Internet.

Switch on a computer, select a search engine and key in the word. Google alone offers over 16,700,000 sites to choose from! Hitting on one or the other of them will eventually lead to an extraordinary assessment of methods by which the future may be foretold. What follows was compiled by an organization called BoxArt and is reproduced here with its generous permission.

## Aeromancy

This form of divination looks to the air and sky for inspiration, particularly concerning itself with cloud shapes, comets and other phenomenon not normally visible in the heavens (see also Meteoromancy).

## Alchemy

The much sought after but never achieved practice of transmutation of base metals into precious metals (e.g. gold or silver) with the aid of an esoteric third substance is a form of divination, seeking as it does to use 'divine' knowledge to alter things.

## Alectryomancy

Those who divine by alectryomancy encourage a bird to pick grains of corn from a circle of letters. The letter closest to the grain pecked is noted and the words eventually formed used as an augury. A variation is to intone the letters of the alphabet at sunrise, noting those at which the cock crows.

## Aleuromancy

Anyone who has ever eaten a fortune cookie has knowingly or unknowingly indulged in aleuromancy whereby answers to questions are rolled into balls of dough, which once baked are chosen at random by those who have questions to ask.

## Alomancy

Also known as halomancy, this form of divination involves studying the patterns made by table salt poured from the hand of the practitioner onto a consecrated surface or small area of land preferably used only for the purpose of divination.

## Alphitomancy

Baking is the media by which some diviners look to find the truth. Specially baked cakes are fed to those who stand accused of a misdeed of some sort, to establish guilt or innocence. The cakes are digestible by someone with a clear conscience but are unpleasant to those with guilt written on their minds.

## Anthropomancy

Now long-outlawed, anthropomancy is a means of divination that involves human sacrifice.

## Apantomancy

The chance meeting with animals such as black cats, many types of birds and other creatures is believed by some to be a sign of things to come. The siting of Mexico

City was a result of apantomancy. According to legend, Aztec practitioners of the art saw an eagle, a live snake in its mouth, soar into the air from the cactus on which it had been perched, and took this as a sign that such a spot would be the place around which to built a settlement!

## Astraglomancy

Sometimes known as astragyromancy, this method of selecting a path through the future uses special dice that bear numbers and letters on their sides.

## Astrology

Those who practise this, one of the oldest, most popular and scientific forms of divination, look to the Sun, the Moon, the planets and the stars, and their position and passage through the sky to tell on whom the Sun will be shining in future. The Babylonians practised the art, and it is more or less accepted by most people who have looked at the relevant research with an open mind that the Great Pyramid and other mausoleums in the Nile Valley were built with astrology very much in mind.

## Austromancy

The way the wind is blowing is believed by some to provide a guide as to what prevailing currents hold in store in days to come.

## Axiomancy

When an axe or hatchet is driven into a post, the way in which it quivers before settling is thought to provide a signpost to what will occur in the days to follow.

## Belomancy

Similar to axiomancy (see above) the ancient art of belomancy looks to the flight of arrows and how they move when they hit their target to point the way to what lies ahead.

## Bibliomancy

Diviners who practise this particular skill use books to thumb their way through the library of the future. A question is asked, the chosen book is opened at random, and the words on which the eye first falls are then interpreted to answer the enquirer.

## Botanomancy

Botanomancers look to the shapes made in wood and leaf fires to discern future events.

## Capnomancy

One stage on from botanomancy, capnomancy concerns itself with interpreting the forms taken on by smoke swirling upwards from a fire to help them peer through the veil that shrouds the future from the eyes of non-believers.

## Cartomancy

Competing with astrology for the Number One spot in the top twenty of divination (in the West at least), cartomancy in any of its several forms uses cards to answer the questions that those who wish to look into the future ask. The cards may by those in an ordinary playing pack, or a specially designed one such as the Tarot.

## Catoptomancy

This early form of crystal gazing catches moonbeams in a mirror turned towards the Moon and interprets the shapes and patterns they create to form a picture of future events and to answer questions as to which is the best path to tread through them.

## Causiomancy

When an object is placed in a fire, it may burn, melt, change colour, evaporate and move or behave in a variety of ways. Causiomancers gaze into the flames at objects cast into them and draw their conclusions from they way they react to the melting heat.

## Cephalomancy

The root of the word, the Latin 'cephalicus', itself derived from the Greek word for 'head' (kefáli), provides the inspiration for this particular type of divination, but gives no clue to as to which particular type of head. In fact, those who divine via cephalomancy use the heated skull or head of a donkey or goat as the key that unlocks the door to future events.

## Ceraunomancy

Many ancient peoples believed that thunder and lightning were one of the ways in which the gods communicated with each other. And as the gods were omnipotent, what better way to divine the future than to eavesdrop on their conversations, using thunderclaps and lightning flashes to give ceraunomancers the gift of foresight?

## Ceromancy

Also known as ceroscopy, ceromancy practitioners pour molten wax into water and use the shapes taken on by the hardening substance as the clues that will unravel the mysteries of the future.

## Chiromancy

Closely allied to palmistry, (see below) chiromancy concerns itself only with the lines of the hands to discern what tomorrow has in its grip, whereas the former uses other features of the hand to find out what lies in store.

## Chirognomy

Like palmistry (see below) this is another way of divining the future by observing the hand. Chirognomancers study its general formation rather than the more particular aspects considered by chiromancers and palmists.

## Clairaudience

The word means 'clear hearing'. This method of divination is usually regarded as a form of extrasensory perception (ESP) whereby the unseen spirits who inhabit the future 'speak' to the select band who have 'the gift'.

## Clairvoyance

Using their gift, which is another form of ESP, clairvoyants 'see' into the future, either during a self-induced trance during which pictures of future events come to mind, or in flashes that can come, unsettlingly, out of the blue. According to one claim, a passenger about to embark on the RMS *Titanic* had one such sudden clairvoyant experience as she was about to board the doomed liner and refused to sail.

## Cleromancy

The shifting patterns of sea shells and pebbles on the beach, either moved by the flowing tide or taken from an appropriate beach and dropped from the hands of the diviner, are believed by cleromancers to help them dip into the waters of tomorrow. Another method of cleromancy is to hold a seashell up to the ear and listen. Most of us, when children, did this and were convinced we could hear the sea. Cleromancers with an ear for this sort of thing, believe that the gentle rushing that can sometimes be heard is a voice from the future telling of events yet to happen or trends that will gradually unfold as the tide of life ebbs and flows.

## Clidomancy

Also known as cleidomancy, clidomancy uses the twistings and twirlings of a key suspended from a specially blessed or charmed cord to open the portal that shields the forthcoming (see also Radiesthesia).

## Coscinomancy

Whereas clidomancers use a key, coscinomancers use a suspended sieve to solve the riddle of what is around the corners we must turn as we move through our lives (see also Radiesthesia).

## Critomancy

This comparatively (very!) obscure method of peeking into the future involves baking special barley cakes. The way they take shape in the oven and the patterns the crumbs make when the cakes are being eaten, are the things that those who bake them hold to be significant.

## Cromniomancy

Not much is known about this old method of divination other than that onion sprouts were thought to be able to provide pointers to the future.

## Crystallomancy

When we think of divination or, to give it its more common name, fortune telling, one of the images that comes to mind is probably that of an old woman peering into her crystal ball and via it into things to come. Fortune tellers are crystallomancers by another name. It need not be a crystal ball: any crystal on which the seer is properly focused can be used. Some crystals are said to have special powers and are used for their own purpose. Sunstone, for example, is reputed to be an excellent conduit for those seeking knowledge of future matters of a sexual nature, while rose quartz has the reputation for helping those seeking advice on how to mend quarrels especially with those close to them.

## Cyclomancy

The behaviour of a turning wheel, how long it goes round for and the directions or things to which its spokes are pointing when it comes or is brought to a halt, are all scrutinized by cyclomancers in their search for answers as to what's going to happen during future spins of the wheel of life.

## Dactylomancy

This is a branch of radiethesia (see below) that uses a ring suspended on a piece of string or specially consecrated cord to peer into the mists of time to come.

## Daphnomancy

People who divine using daphnomancy as their chosen method do so by burning laurel branches on an open fire and interpreting the resulting crackling that fills the air. Laurel is a wood that was sacred to the Ancient Greeks, who believed that it communicated the spirit of prophecy.

## Dendromancy

Like daphnomancy (see above) wood is the key to this method of divination, in this case either oak or mistletoe. The former was sacred to the God of Thunder because it was thought to be the most likely tree in the forest to be struck by lightning and was therefore a conduit to him, and thence to others in the pantheon. Mistletoe was held in great veneration by the Druids and, later, was thought to be the wood from which Christ's cross was made.

## Dowsing

This is the method by which the presence of water or precious metals is divined by using a forked rod that vibrates when held over the spot where what is being searched for is to be found. Hazel is the favoured wood for the purpose. Many people scoff at the very idea of dowsing, but there are too many records of times when it has been used successfully to detect water when all other methods have failed, for it to be derided by non-believers.

## Geloscopy

This curious way of divination uses the tone of laughter as the way to find out what is about to happen to whoever is amused.

## Genethialogy

This is the branch of astrology that predicts the path a person's life will take by plotting the positions of the stars and planets in the various astrological houses at the time of birth. It is one of the few methods of divination that lends itself to twenty-first-century technology! Anyone who wants to use genethialogy to find out their destiny needs only access a suitable website, and key in where and exactly when they were born. Once credit card details have been cleared, a detailed analysis will come on screen, which is simply downloaded to be constantly at hand.

## Graphology

Handwriting has long been held to provide a key to character analysis. Indeed, some firms have such a strong belief in graphology, that they will not offer employment to anyone whose handwriting does not come up to scratch. Of course, if you know what characteristics are desired, with a little work you could ensure your success.

## Gyromancy

This is a particularly active form of divination whereby the diviner walks around a circle, marked with letters at various points around its circumference, until dizziness sets in. This causes the diviner to stumble at different points, the letters at these points eventually spelling out a prophecy.

## Haruspication

Perhaps one of the most famous of the ancient methods of divination, haruspication involves inspecting the entrails of an animal. It was widely practised by priests in ancient Rome: Shakespearean scholars will recall that in *The Tragedy of Julius Caesar*, the eponymous hero's wife, Calpurnia, warns him not to go to the Senate on the fateful Ides of March because of what has been foretold by priests who used this art.

## Hieromancy

Also known as hierscopy, hieromancy is divination by observing objects of sacrifice – how they move in their death throes, how the blood flows and the shape the eventually lifeless form takes. It is now illegal in most parts of the world, but is probably still performed in regions where animism is the prevailing religion.

## Hippomancy

Hippomancers divine the future by watching horses, taking note especially of their stomping and neighing. The art was probably developed among tribes of Native Americans and was observed by settlers on the trek west as still being practised by native tribes well into the nineteenth century.

## Horoscopy

This is more or less another name for astrology, involving the use of astrological horoscopes to divine the future.

## Hydromancy

Watching the water – its colour, ebb and flow, and the ripples produced by pebbles dropped in a pool – is the source of inspiration behind this particular form of divination. Usually, but not necessarily the water was contained in a pool dedicated to one or other of the pantheon in which the seer believed.

## Icthyomancy

Believers in icthyomancy think that by watching the way a fish behaves when it is placed in a consecrated pool, they, too, can swim in the waters of knowledge of tomorrow.

## Lampadomancy

The way that the flames of torches used specifically for lampadomancy flicker allows those who practise this divinatory art to shed light on the events of tomorrow and the days thereafter.

## Lecanomancy

Lecanomancers gaze into a basin of water in much the same way that crystallomancers (see above) focus on their crystals hoping that as they reflect on their own or their followers' questions, the answers will be revealed.

## Libanomancy

As incense burns, the fumes given off twist and turn in the air, creating endlessly fascinating patterns. It is these patterns that libanomancers observe, hoping to see in them the solutions to whatever it is that troubles them.

## Lithomancy

Precious stones have long fascinated humankind, and it is little surprise, therefore, to learn that they were – and still are – used in divination. With their own powers and colours, gemstones can be used by lithomancers to gaze into many aspects of the future.

## Margaritomancy

Margaritomancers hold a pearl in their hands, think deeply of the questions they want answered, and drop it on to a solid surface. The way it bounces and how it rolls and comes to rest, give those who seek to know, their insights into the future!

## Metagnomy

Many seers fall into a trance during which they have visions of the future. Many clairvoyants do this, as do practitioners of many kinds of divination. Metagnomy is a general term for this divination derived from visions received during a trance.

## Meteoromancy

Today, most people (in the western world at least) know that meteors are small pieces of space debris that burn up on entering the Earth's atmosphere and produce shooting stars. Lacking this knowledge, our ancestors regarded them as portents of future events. This belief lingers on, not just in developing lands, meteoromancers believing that these pyrotechnic phenomena can illumine the future.

## Metoposcopy

Whereas phrenology (see below) concerns itself with the shape of the skull to give practitioners of the art a head start in future events, metoposcopy considers that the lines of the forehead are what matters when assessing a person's character and hence gaining an insight into what could await the sitter.

## Molybdomancy

When lead is heated to liquid form, a loud hissing emanates from the melting pot. According to molybdomancers those who inhabit the spirit world and know what the future holds communicate this knowledge to those in tune with them via this medium.

## Myomancy

The manner in which several of the thousands of rats and mice (the most numerous family of all mammals) scurry hither and thither in response to various stimuli tells those who practise myomancy the course of future events. Cynics may say that when they perceive rats leaving a ship, it is pretty obvious that the boat is about to sink! But in parts of the world where people are more in tune with nature than the city sophisticates of the western world, rodent behaviour is regarded as a means of divining the future.

## Numerology

One of the best known methods of divination, numerology divines by interpreting numbers, dates and the numerical value of letters. Numbers were used for divination by the Ancient Chinese and Egyptians, but it was in Classical Greece and among the Hebrews that numerology was developed, Pythagoras, for example, believing that numbers were, 'the first things in Nature'.

## Oculomancy

The eyes, it is said, are the keys to the soul. They are also, according to oculomancy, a reliable guide to a person's character and when focused on by a practised oculomancer can provide clues as to what they will behold in the future.

## Oenomancy

Wine is not only pleasant to drink, oenomancers believe that when poured into special chalices and gazed into, what they see will uncork future events. It can also be poured from the chalice and the patterns it forms can, to experienced eyes, yield clues to tomorrow's world.

## Omphalomancy

This particular method of divination has but one use only – to foretell the number of subsequent children women will have by counting the knots on the umbilical cord following the arrival of the firstborn.

## Oneiromancy

Dream interpretation's proper name, oneiromancy must be a contender for the oldest form of divination. Maybe the most famous of those with the gift of telling dreamers what their nocturnal imaginings meant is Joseph, whose adventures are related in the Old Testament Book of Genesis. And perhaps the most amusing comment on this was made by Sir Tim Rice who, in the lyrics of *Joseph and His Amazing Technicolour Dreamcoat*, has Joseph interpreting the Pharaoh's dream in the words, 'All those things you saw in your pyjamas, were the long-range forecast for the farmers.'

## Onomancy

Names are the driving force behind this method of divination, which has its roots in numerology (see above). The letters they contain and the syllables they form are ascribed values that combine to enable the seer to plot the course to take.

## Onychomancy

This branch of the art of palmistry (see below) concentrates on the fingernails – their shape length and other features – rather than the whole hand, to fulfil its divinatory function. There is a definite scientific base to part of onychomancy as the colour of a person's nails can be indicative of certain conditions: for example, nails that have a hint of yellow about them may suggest liver problems.

## Oomantia

Oomantia (also known as ooscopy and ovamancy), is a method of divination that uses eggs rolled on the ground, spun round or simply passed from the hand of those who have questions to the hand of those with answers as its inspiration. The diviner may simply observe the egg, grasp it hoping to feel vibrations, or hold it to his ear.

## Opiomancy

The hissing of snakes, the way they move along the ground and respond to what they encounter is the basis of this serpentine method of divination.

## Orniscopy

Sometimes known as orinthomancy, this is a branch of apantomancy (see above). It uses the behaviour and movements of birds, particularly those in the air, to enable diviners to take a flight into the future to see what it holds both for themselves and those who seek to gain from their gifts. Shakespeare mentions divination by this method in *The Tragedy of Julius Caesar* when he has Casca bid his fellow conspirators to heed . . .

> *. . . the bird of night [that] did sit*
> *Even at noon-day, upon the market-place,*
> *Hooting and shrieking.*

## Palmistry

Experts in this ancient art use the lines, mounds and shape of the hands, fingers and nails as the basis for their assessments of the character and future developments of those having their palm read. The mounds (or mounts) are each linked with one or other of the planets, marrying palmistry and the equally old art of astrology (see above) in happy unison.

## Pegomancy

Spring water and the way it bubbles up through natural fountains are used by pegomancers to discern how those who seek the way ahead should take the plunge.

## Phrenology

One of the oldest methods of divination, phrenology uses the shape of the head and the small mounds and depression on the skull to give a character reading and to foretell the future of those who want to know what awaits them as they tread their way along the bumpy path of life.

## Phyllorhodmancy

This charming method of divining the future involves a rose petal being slapped against the face of the person who would know what will grow in the garden that is the future. The diviner listens carefully for the sound that results from the floral assault and bases his or her auguries on it!

## Physiognomy

Practitioners of this art study the physical features of the faces of those who seek their wisdom to analyze their characters, which, some believe, may provide a pointer to what is in store.

## Physchography

Physchographers are in tune with a spiritual force that 'tells' those blessed with the gift messages to write down, sometimes but not always, when the seer is in a trance. There are many recorded cases of this 'automatic writing' including several whereby dead composers have used the medium of a living person as the chalice whereby they can carry on their work from beyond the grave.

## Pyramancy

Also known as pyroscopy, pyramancy is a general term for divining the future by studying fire and flame. Divination is often assisted by throwing substances onto the flames (see also botanomancy, capnomancy, causiomancy, daphamancy, lampadomancy and libanomancy, and xylomancy).

## Radiesthesia

This is a general term for divination that uses a device such as a divining rod or pendulum.

## Rhapsodomancy

This rather romantic method of divination uses poetry as its inspiration, Those with the gift of rhapsodamancy use a book of verse opened at random and a chance-chosen passage on that page as their way of divining future chapters in life's tome. The practice is a branch of stichomancy (see below) and bibliomancy (see above).

## Sciomancy

Sciomancers are mediums by another name – people with the gift of communicating with the spirit guides who inhabit the unseen world, usually when in a trance-like state.

## Scrying

Whole books have been written about scrying, an all-encompassing term for divination via a wide of assortment of aids from smoke to shells to induce visions that tell what the gods have in store for us.

## Sideromancy

This rare, but still-practised form of divination is, like so many, pagan in origin. Sideromancers use a hot iron to set straw a-smouldering, and study the various shapes the stalks adopt as they slowly catch fire. They also consider the way any smoke given off twists and spirals upwards, interpreting what they see through the haze to give them insights into tomorrow's world.

## Sortilege

Those who practise sortilege cast lots and use the shapes in which they fall as the basis of their omens. The lots can take several forms – animal, vegetable and mineral. There are many versions of sortilege, which have been given their own names, which are too various to detail here but can be found online.

## Spodomancy

Our ancient ancestors understandably held fire in some awe. They used it to heat their primitive dwellings, cook their food and guard them from marauding animals. It is little wonder then that fire is involved in some way in so many forms of divination. This particular one involves deciphering the patterns seen in cinders and soot to peer into the inglenooks of tomorrow.

## Stichomancy

A branch of divination that, like rhapsodomancy, uses the printed word to turn pages of the upcoming chapters in the Book of Life. But whereas the latter relies on poetry, stichomancy can be done with any book (see also Bibliomancy).

## Stolisomancy

This curious (but perhaps no more curious than others) method of telling the future considers that the way people dress holds the clue not just to their character, but also to their future. There is probably something in the argument that what one chooses to wear in the morning does reflect the way one feels, and wearing certain colours might affect one's mood, so perhaps this particular form of divination should be regarded with more respect than it is in some quarters.

## Sycomancy

This sylvan form of divination is performed by writing various prophecies or different answers to the same question on tree leaves, and leaving them to dry naturally. Whatever is written on the last leaf to dry is most likely to come true. A more modern version requires those seeking what they wish for the future to write their desires on slips of paper which are then rolled up and, along with one blank rolled piece, put in a strainer and held over a boiling pot. The first to unroll is, it is believed, the wish that will come true. If the blank one unrolls before the others it is a warning that there is no point in proceeding with the divination at this particular moment in time.

## Tasseography

Reading the leaves is one of the most popular forms of amateur divination. After the tea has been enjoyed, the cup is placed upside down on the saucer to drain it completely, and the shapes formed by the leaves are interpreted as pointers to the way things will be. The origins of reading the leaves are obscure, but it is known to have been practised in China for thousands of years, which is hardly surprising as tea-drinking was common there for many millennia before it spread to other countries.

## Tiromancy

Cheese and the crumbs it leaves on the plate may seem unlikely pointers to the future, but in the world of divination, there is little that cannot be used as indicative of things to come – and what's on the cheeseboard or growing on the cheese is no exception.

## Xylomancy

The shapes of pieces of wood when they are collected and the way this changes when the logs are burned is the basis on which xylomancers make their predictions as to how to cope with any future knotty problems (see pyromancy above).

In an ideal world, each one of these different methods of divination would be given equal space. We would look at the history of them all, where they were or still are practised, and how effective they are. Sadly, we don't live in an ideal world. Instead, we will concentrate on the ones with which most of us have come in contact, or which are accessible to us.

Cynics will say that divination in these and its other myriad forms is a load of pie in the sky: everyone is entitled to their own opinion. But others, perhaps more open-minded souls, will pause for a moment before they join the ranks of the disbelievers. They would be wise to do so, for there is a considerable body of evidence in favour of those who are certain that there is something in it.

Of course, no one (at least no one sensible) would claim that the old lady who sets up a stall at the vicar's fête and charges good-natured villagers a pound to peer into her crystal ball and tell their future is doing anything else than raising some much-needed cash for the restoration fund. And when she has a friend round for tea and offers to 'read your cup, dear,' no one really believes that she has 'the gift'.

But what about the well-documented case of the seven-year-old girl whose mother slept during the day and kept watch all night when sailing on a cross-Atlantic liner because she 'knew' it was going to sink? The mother was called Esther and young girl's name was Eva Hart... and the ship was the RMS *Titanic*.

Or Jeanne Dixon, one of the United States' most celebrated clairvoyants. In 1956 she foretold that a Democratic president with 'thick brown hair and blue eyes', would be assassinated by a man whose name began with O or Q. Seven years later, John F. Kennedy, the thick-brown haired, blue-eyed Democratic President was assassinated in Dallas, Texas by a man whose name began with an O – Lee Harvey Oswald.

As Hamlet said, 'There are more things in heaven and earth, Horatio, than are dreamt of in your philosophy.'

Successful divination is one of them.

# It's on the cards

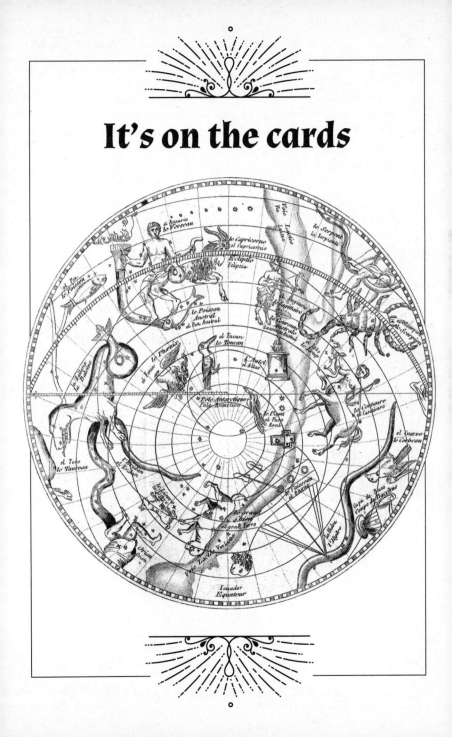

The history of playing cards is lost in the mists of time. Some claim they were the invention of the Ancient Chinese, others that they were first used in Ancient Egypt. India has also been put forward as the place whence they originated. There are perhaps links with the Crusaders who may have learned about them from the Saracens, who may have used them to divine the future since the eighth century AD and there may be a connection with the Knights Templar! The truth? We shall probably never know.

What we do know is there are, in the Bibliothèque Nationale in Paris, seventeen cards, sixteen of which are recognizably Tarot in origin. It was once thought that these dated from the reign of Charles VI (1368-1422), the French king who lost the Battle of Agincourt and died insane. But recent research suggests that they are Italian, taking the name 'Tarot' from the river Taro, a tributary of the Po.

The Tarot is the forerunner of the modern playing pack. The earliest complete pack, painted by Italian Renaissance artist Bonifacio Bembo, is now in the J. Pierpoint Morgan Library in New York: the cards are bear a strong resemblance to the modern Tarot deck.

As the modern playing pack gradually evolved from the Tarot, the names of the suits – Cups (sometimes called Chalices), Wands (Batons), Pentacles (Coins) and Swords evolved (in the English pack) to Hearts, Clubs, Diamonds and Spades.

Both the Tarot and the ordinary pack can be used to divine the future.

Many are the ways of laying out a pack. The simplest is the *Three Spread* – the first card represents the past and is placed at the left of the surface. The second card (the present) placed to the right of the first and the third (the future) to the right of the second.

In the *Year Ahead* spread, twelve cards are laid clockwise, the first at twelve o'clock. The fourth card is laid alongside the third and fifth cards (the third lying directly under the fifth) and the tenth one alongside the ninth and the eleventh, that card lying directly above the ninth. The *Year Ahead* spread shows current influences and those that will influence the questioner over the next twelve months. It offers a good general view of what lies in store.

The *Horoscope* spread is based on the twelve houses of the Zodiac. The first card is laid at nine o'clock, the second at eight o'clock and so on with the twelfth card at ten o'clock. This spread is often used to focus on potential, character and as a pointer to relationships and career. The areas each card covers are as follows:

| First | Personality. |
| Second | Personal values and monetary matters. |
| Third | Communications and short journeys. |
| Fourth | Home and family. |
| Fifth | Romance, creativity and children. |
| Sixth | Vocation and health. |
| Seventh | Relationships. |
| Eighth | Shared resources. |
| Ninth | Long journeys and matters philosophical. |
| Tenth | Career goals and aspirations. |
| Eleventh | Friends and hopes. |
| Twelveth | Unconscious mind and hidden limitations. |

The *Yes or No* spread is a diagonal cross, with the first card at the centre of the cross. Running downwards

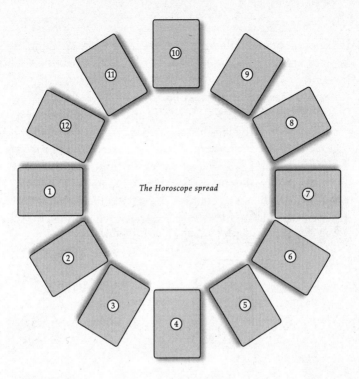

*The Horoscope spread*

from top left to bottom right, the order of the cards is as follows – fifth, fourth, first, third and second. And upwards from bottom left to top right sixth, seventh, first, eighth and ninth. The spread is designed to give a straightforward 'Yes!' or 'No!' answer to a question. An upright first card is a 'Yes!' a reversed one a 'No!' Cards two and three indicate helpful influences, cards four and five, the questioner's mental reaction, cards six and seven the adverse influences, and cards eight and nine the emotional reaction.

*The Celtic Cross* is one of the most widely used, being the most general and non-specific of layouts, showing the history behind the question, current influences, hurdles that have to be cleared, social factors and the likely

*The Celtic Cross*

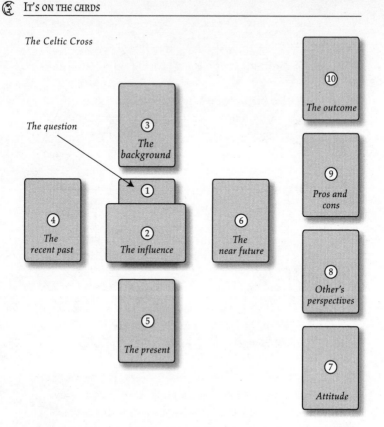

outcome. Answers to questions are valid for three months, past or future. The first card is positioned vertically in the centre, the second horizontally along the bottom of the first. The third card is above these two and the fourth alongside to the left. The fifth card is positioned below the central three, the sixth on the right of them. Cards seven, eight, nine and ten lie in a vertical line to the right of the sixth, the seventh at the bottom of the column, the tenth at the top. The areas the cards cover are:

First        The question – describing the nature of the
             question and the motive behind it.

Second        The influence – the atmosphere, personalities or emotions that have a bearing on the question.

Third         The background – the history, events and relationships that have led to the question being asked.

Fourth        The recent past – something that has just happened that has a direct influence on the question.

Fifth         The present – the current state of the questioner – hopes, fears and emotions.

Sixth         The near future.

Seventh       Attitude – the way in which the questioner approaches the subject of the question.

Eighth        Other's perspectives – the feeling of those close to the questioner about what is being asked.

Ninth         Pros and cons – a cool, detached analysis of the question.

Tenth         The outcome.

The *Gypsy* spread is one of the most common non-Tarot layouts. Revealing past and present influences, hidden as well as visible, it is best used to find out what lies behind a particular situation as well as helping to see into the future and to give some indication of when. The cards are laid out in three columns of seven cards each, starting at the top left and working across to form seven rows of three cards each. The rows have the following relevance:

| Top Row | The self and what is stirring within. |
| Second | Environment and relationships. |
| Third | Hope, fears and desires. |
| Fourth | Expectations. |
| Fifth | Destiny and hidden influences. |
| Sixth | The next three months. |
| Seventh | The following quarter. |

Some card readers keep two sets of cards – one for doing personal readings, one for divining for others. In the latter case a significator card is often used to represent the questioner. This may be chosen at random or if doing a Tarot reading, according to the correspondences that should be explained in the pack.

Many card readers keep their cards in a specially consecrated box or silk bag or pouch. Some insist that the pack is shuffled in a certain way and that it is given and received with the left hand only, or the right. There are no hard-and-fast rules. Or if there is one it is that if it is right for you, then it is the right way for you to do it.

# The Tarot

The Tarot pack comprises seventy-eight cards – fifty-six Minor Arcana, divided into the four suits, and twenty-two pictorial cards, the Major Arcana, numbered 0 to 21. The suits of the Minor Arcana represented the different strata of society – Cups were the clergy, Wands the peasants, Pentacles the tradesmen and Swords were the aristocracy.

Today with hundreds of different designs to chose from, it might seem difficult for the beginner to decide which one to select. There are those who believe that it is unlucky to choose your own pack. But most of us ignore this and, quite rightly, let our instincts decide the pack to use. Rightly? Because instinct is all when it comes to the Tarot. Each card has its own meaning, influenced by the way the cards present themselves and the way in which they are laid out, but it is the diviner's instinct that is perhaps the most important element of any reading. Also, there are special Tarot packs for special purposes: there's a Lover's pack that is often used to answer questions concerning love, sex and relationships. There are packs that combine astrology with the Tarot. And there is a Witchcraft pack – the Aleister Crowley Thoth pack – each card related in some way to witchcraft and black magic.

Before the cards are laid out, they must by shuffled. The most common way is to shuffle the cards whole, focusing the mind on the question to the exclusion of everything else. The pack is now cut into three piles, which are placed in front of the reader who picks up the last cut pile and places it on top of the first pile, then stacks the second pile on top of that. The cards are then dealt face down in the chosen spread. Another way is to fan the cards out after they have been shuffled and to draw out the number of cards required at random, turning the cards over as they are read. Card readers sometimes use only the Major Arcana, in which case only these cards are shuffled.

Each of the cards in the pack has its own meaning – one for when it is drawn properly and one when it is reversed. The suits, too, have their own correspondences, which are significant when many cards of the same suit turn up in a spread:

| | | | |
|---|---|---|---|
| *Wands* | Work, creativity, reputation, fame, enterprise and efficiency. | | |
| *Cups* | Love, happiness, harmony, sensitivity, fertility and unity. | | |
| *Swords* | Ideas and communications, hostility, struggle, bitterness and malice. | | |
| *Pentacles* | Money, stability and material matters. | | |

And the lower cards of the Minor Arcana can be used to give some indication of time.

| | Swords | Wands | Cups | Pentacles |
|---|---|---|---|---|
| 2 | March | June | September | December |
| 3 | April | July | October | January |
| 4 | May | August | November | February |

# The Major Arcana

Names can vary from pack to pack, but the numbers are a constant. Major because they are concerned with deeper issues than the Minor cards, these twenty-two cards represent the innermost qualities of the questioner's psyche and personality.

0   *The Fool*, often depicted standing on the edge of a precipice, bag and rose in hand and with a dog snapping at his legs. Drawing it suggests that a choice must by made and it is time to face up to reality.

Reversed it indicates indecisiveness, irresponsibility and madness.

1   *The Magician*, wand in hand, serpent coiled around his waist in some packs, is a person of authority who brings with him the power to do good. Whoever turns the Magician over is being told that they have the ability to get on in life as long as they realize that obstacles are there to be overcome. Reversed it suggests deviousness, unreliability and a manipulative nature.

2   *The High Priestess*, often depicted as a female pope, tells of knowledge and serenity, wisdom and intuition. But reversed she implies ignorance. When she appears this way in a spread she can be carrying a warning that something is going on behind your back. Be careful in whom you confide.

3   *The Empress*, sitting on her throne, radiates renewal, nurture and nourishment. She can mean marriage and motherhood as well as material gains in the offing. Reversed, she warns of a tendency to put others before oneself with a consequent loss of identity.

4   *The Emperor* is the card of fathering and indicates focus and an energy that gets things done. It indicates that someone in a position of authority will offer advice that should be taken seriously. Reversed it suggests an over-critical, arrogant and impatient nature that can lead to trouble. Heed the warning.

5   *The High Priest* or Pope may be a wise teacher, but he can bring with him an unnecessary desire for social

approval. When reversed, he is saying that there is
an unwillingness to accept change that is preventing
moving ahead in life. His appearance can indicate that
there will be a renewed interest in religion and that
if a new person appears on the horizon, every effort
should be made to impress him or her.

6   *The Lovers*, the card of love and emotion, relationships
and the family. They are the innocent us before we
became sullied by life. They bring in their wake
unification, problems solved and new projects
embraced. Reversed they warn of problems on the love
front and unwelcome choices that have to be made.

7   *The Chariot*, drawn by two wild creatures symbolizing
the will, is a card of challenge, change and eventual
triumph. Obstacles will be overcome by seeing what
has to be done and making sure that it is carried
out. Reversed it cautions against making impulsive
decisions and a tendency to make change for
change's sake.

8   *Justice* is the card of principle and true speaking, of
the desire to do what is right. In its positive guise it
says that in any upcoming brush with officialdom, a
judicious use of facts and accurate detail will ensure
that a just result will ensue. Reversed, it counsels
against accepting injustice in exchange for a quiet life,
even if it means seeing someone being treated unfairly.

9   *The Hermit*, holding up his lamp lit with knowledge
and wisdom and leaning on the staff of experience,
means wisdom and learning gained through living. It
says, 'listen to your inner voice and if it says retreat

from the world for a while to renew creativity' then do just that. Reversed, it suggests that introversion, fraud and deceit will cast their shadow. Its appearance in a spread can mean that it is time to change the course that life is taking and that a move to a new location may be necessary.

10   *The Wheel of Fortune* represents the input of something unexpected – maybe good, maybe bad – on the horizon. In its normal position, it can herald a new opportunity that, if grasped, will lead to nothing but good. Reversed it warns that you are allowing others to have too strong an influence on your life.

11   *Force* or *Strength*, usually showing a woman forcing closed the jaws of a lion, unafraid of the danger, represents the courage to overcome any danger, as well as patience and perseverance. Reversed, though, it suggests that the subject of the reading is scared that plans in the offing will meet with opposition and that little will be done to face it.

12   *The Hanged Man*, the card of sacrifice and the willingness to face short-term losses for long-term gains. This card does not presage loss, but letting go. This is often a decision to make a better life by giving up an immediate advantage. Reversed it shows an unwillingness to let go and a refusal to see the long-term benefits to be had from a recently presented opportunity.

13   *Death*, the Grim Reaper, is a card that tells us of approaching endings that will free us and set us off on new paths, as long as we can accept them. If it appears

reversed, then we face stagnation or unwelcome changes that will see us having to pick our way through an unknown and unwelcoming new landscape.

14  *Temperance* is a card of healing and harmony indicated by the figure pouring water from one vessel to another encouraging us to let the life force flow freely. It counsels us that compromise is the answer to any problems. Reversed it can presage upcoming discord.

15  *The Devil*, the card that represents the instinctual, shadowy part of ourselves, says that something looms, something unavoidable, and that although it may alarm us, all's well that ends well. When it's reversed something that's looming will not turn out well.

16  *The Tower*, struck by lightning and starting to crumble, tells us the unexpected is to be welcomed as it liberates us from stale routine and jaded opinions. Reversal indicates chaos, maybe financial, emotional or even both.

17  *The Star*, symbol of hope, inspiration and rebirth, is seen shining brightly above a beautiful female who is emptying jugs of water into a stream. She promises change for the better unless she is reversed, when disappointment will pour from her pitcher and sully your happiness.

18  *The Moon*, dying in the night sky only to be reborn again a few days later, is concerned with the unconscious and can indicate that occult forces are at work in our lives. Even unreversed it can herald disillusionment; reversed it says confusion will reign

causing us to make mistakes and bring deception into our lives.

19 *The Sun*, seen shining on a child, is symbolic of energy, joy, optimism and worldly success. It says that this is the perfect moment to embrace opportunity. It promises happiness (maybe the birth of a baby) and health. Even reversed it still promises some happiness in all these respects, but it may be clouded by loneliness.

20 *The Last Judgement*, often portrayed by figures rising from their graves, means the end of one phase in life and the start of a new one. But we can only move on after we have taken a good look at the past and forgiven ourselves for mistakes made, which is something that is hard to do. Reversed it presages delays and postponements, and warns of the dangers of acting on hasty judgements.

21 *The World*, seen accompanied by a dancing female, is the card of completion and of expanding horizons. Challenges have been faced. Battles fought and won. New ones beckon and they can be viewed with confidence. When it is found to be reversed, it signifies resistance to change and that there is more than a passing danger of becoming too established in every aspect of life.

## The Minor Arcana

Whereas the cards in the Major Arcana reflect the big issues in life, those in the Minor Arcana show humdrum, day-to-day events and how these affect you. These are the things that comprise most of our lives, and although they may seem insignificant, it is often our reaction to them that sets off major changes.

A Tarot reading that includes the Minor Arcana can reveal many things, including – perhaps most importantly – if your life has become entrenched in a pattern, in which case the cards can help you change repetitive cycles and broaden your outlook. Experience in life can be said to be defined by your feelings at every moment of existence: the cards in the Minor Arcana reflect not just these experiences but the manner in which you externalize them.

As mentioned earlier, the four suits have their own correspondences and can also be used to give some indication of time.

A reversed Minor Arcana card reverses its upright meaning. The damage done by an ominous upright card is undone when it is reversed – but a reversed court card (king, queen, knight, page), in general, is a hostile one.

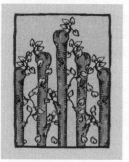

### Wands
*Concerning career and matters creative*

*One*   A card that signifies new beginnings, which will bring changes especially in career matters. It can also presage a birth in the family and that an important communication will be received.

*Two*   This says that when success comes, it will be due to determination. It can also indicate that talks resulting in some kind of partnership are in the offing, and that a document promising some sort of financial security will require your signature.

*Three*    An auspicious card that promises to bless new projects, and says that if you look to the right person for advice, what they say will bring tremendous benefit.

*Four*    Past efforts will bear fruit if not now then soon. The card promises a time of peace and harmony and whispers that romance may be in the air.

*Five*    Not the nicest card in the pack. It says that pressure will build up and may become intolerable, but that if you stand up for what you believe in, things will turn out to your advantage. It also says that to get the cooperation you are going to need, then you must put your cards on the table and tell the truth, the whole truth and nothing but the truth.

*Six*    Good news is winging its way towards you, but it may get blown off course before it gets to you. So don't give up: success will come your way as long as you keep trying. There could be a journey in the offing, and relationships are about to take a turn for the better.

*Seven*    You have been battling against the odds for so long that now is the time to take a break. Do this and the answer to your problems will come to you. So hold on: the future is not as black as it seems.

*Eight*    News coming your way heralds major changes in your life that could involve a journey that is in some way involved with your career. The Eight of Wands also suggests that a new idea could produce excellent results, especially if it involves financial reorganization.

*Nine*    Stick with an idea, but keep an ear open to the advice of others. Although you have come a long way, you don't have all the answers. But you will have if you listen to what others are saying to you.

*Ten*     You may well have been feeling that you have had the weight of the world on your shoulders and that the recent past has been a whirlwind of constant change. Relax. The burden will soon be shifted and you can view the future, confident that everything will soon settle down.

## Cups
*To do with love and pleasure, sensitivity and fertility*

*One*     Things on the domestic front are about to change for the better, and may involve a move to a new home. Someone new may enter your life and the attraction you feel for them will be intense.

*Two*     A new affair perhaps, certainly a new friendship, is about to perk you up, and the cooperation you receive from someone will give you a tremendous boost.

*Three*     A card that says there will be a happy gathering of people, and that can also herald a complete change in lifestyle. This card often appears just before news of a pregnancy is received.

*Four*     For some reason, and no one knows what, you are feeling unhappy and bored with your lot. This may make you develop a careless attitude towards life and encourage emotional discontent.

*Five*    An unfortunate card that presages a break-up in a marriage or long-term partnership. The card warns you to think carefully before reaching any decision, for the effect could have unforeseen consequences for you or someone you love.

*Six*    An old friend, maybe more than one, will re-enter your life, bringing with him or her, perhaps, a chance to change jobs. And an acquaintance who has recently become a friend could well turn out to have a surprising amount in common with you.

*Seven*    You have a very important decision to make – one that sees you standing on the brink of a new life cycle – and there appears to be more than one option open to you. If you use logic and common sense, the careful decision you come to will enable you to enter that new cycle brimful with confidence.

*Eight*    You seem to be bored and dissatisfied with your lot, maybe because your long-laid plans seem to be stuck in the mire. This could make you want to try something new. But what? Aye there's the rub.

*Nine*    Your health is great, your problems seem to evaporate almost as soon as they appear. If emotional joy and material gain are not yours at present, they soon will be.

*Ten*    A sudden wind of change will bring you more happiness that you thought was possible. It could be meeting the person you want to spend the rest of your life with. If you already have, then your dreams and goals are getting closer by the day.

## Swords
*Ideas and communication to the fore*

*One*   Make long-term plans now and they will come to successful fruition, so shrug off the cloak of pessimism that you have been wearing for far too long. Remember that the past is the past, it's the future that counts. Embrace it.

*Two*   A card that heralds a time when many decisions may have to be made, none of which are easy, and one of which could help you build on the success you have achieved. But which one? The Two of Swords can also presage an upsetting communication.

*Three*   Not a nice card. Family quarrels and squabbles are in the air, and could become so intense that a separation of some kind results. As Noël Coward wrote, 'There are bad times just around the corner . . .' But don't despair. Remember that in Tarot, the other cards in a layout have their own influences and that these can temper things.

*Four*   There *is* light at the end of the tunnel. In fact, you can probably already see it. But don't rush towards it. Think carefully about the moves you have to make to get there. Change, inevitable change, may be in the air. Don't worry. Use it as the foundation stone for future plans and they will succeed.

*Five*   There could be a permanent break-up just around the corner, caused by someone you know taking off in a totally new and unexpected direction. This card can also warn that something you value materially could be lost or stolen.

*Six* You may well be feeling as if every ounce of strength has been sapped from you, having been through a really tough time. But things are reaching a climax, particularly at work. The card can say that a relationship is about to come to an end, and that a long journey might be in the offing.

*Seven* Setbacks will hit the plans that you have made, meaning that they don't turn out as you had hoped. But these setbacks are beyond your control so perhaps the best plan is to change direction and look at all the alternatives.

*Eight* If you are feeling a little below par, remember that a problem shared is a problem halved. You can't make constructive decisions on your own, so ask for advice. Restrictions of some sort may be causing, or are about to cause you concern.

*Nine* An unfortunate card, suggesting serious illness to someone close to you. And if you think that's bad enough, it isn't. There is more bad news on the way.

*Ten* Present circumstances may be making you feel depressed and unhappy. Plans are falling through and you don't understand why. The card can also suggest a long journey and that a legal matter looms large on the horizon.

## Pentacles
*Matters financial, economic and concerning stability*

*One*   Things are looking up. An important document or perhaps another sort of communication will form the basis of a new beginning. A legal matter may well be made to work to your advantage.

*Two*   Good news is winging its way to you and changes are in the offing that will leave you with more than one alternative. Some people may try to influence you and, when you have made your mind up, try to put you off the decision you eventually come to. Don't listen to them.

*Three*   You have worked hard for it, and now your abilities are about to be rewarded. Financial affairs will blossom, especially if you work in a large organization.

*Four*   There's a whiff of change in the air – change for the better, putting you in command of things, able to do whatever you think is best. And not only will a decision regarding finances made now pay dividends, but you could also be about to receive a generous gift.

*Five*   You may feel like giving up. Don't! Hang on in there: you are on the threshold of a major accomplishment. But, some sort of legal wrangle could leave you feeling depressed and facing a loss of some kind. And remember to look after yourself: you may have been neglecting your health recently.

*Six*     The plans and hope you have for the future look good. An opportunity for promotion could present itself to your long-term financial gain.

*Seven*   Be patient. There's a change in the offing and it could come suddenly. Important decisions will have to be made, so plan carefully when making them, and if you are involved in discussions of any kind, you can be confident that things will turn out satisfactorily.

*Eight*   If you have an idea, develop it: it could lead to you learning a new skill that you can use to your long-term advantage. And if you are going through a sticky patch financially, don't worry too much: there will be a steady improvement.

*Nine*    You will achieve your material goals, but be careful that you don't do so at the expense of emotional security. Strike a balance. All the money in the world can't compensate for emotional bankruptcy.

*Ten*     There's all-round improvement in your life. Recognition of your abilities will lead to promotion with the accompanying rise in salary. If you have any emotional problems, they will work themselves out, but you may need to be patient before they do.

## The court cards

There are sixteen court cards in the Tarot pack, each suit having a king, a queen, a knight and a page. The kings are mature males, authority figures who embody power and paternalism, achievement and responsibility. If a king appears in a spread and is not recognized, it might represent your own desires and ambitions. Reversed, they become domineering and inflexible.

Queens are mother figures and, like the kings, figures of authority with inherent fertility and wisdom. When an unrecognized queen turns up, she can stand for your nurturing side in relationships, your motives and intentions. Reversed she has a tendency to possessiveness and to live vicariously.

Knights are young men and women who are on the verge but who have not achieved full emotional security. One who appears unrecognized may represent an uncharacteristic quality that is slowly developing in the querent, be it you or another. Immaturity and a tendency to pursue desires at the expense of others are indicated by a reversed knight.

Pages refer to children or young teenagers of either sex and might represent tentative ambitions, youthful dreams and other undeveloped aspects of the querent's personality. Reversed, they indicate childishness in any person, regardless of age.

*The King of Wands* is a mature man of vision, filled with energy and only too happy to share his wisdom with others. He enjoys life and expects others to do the same. Reversed, though, he presents a selfish face to the world and his loyalty becomes open to question.

*The Queen of Wands* is a wise woman, independent and authoritative, imaginative and intuitive. She has a strong personality and is only too happy to give assistance – but she has to be asked first. When she is reversed, she becomes impatient with those who show weakness and is reluctant to let others take the lead.

*The Knight of Wands* is a great communicator with a love of travel and risk. His powers of innovation allow him to devise brilliant schemes. But reversed he can be mendacious and the sort of person who flits from project to project, starting many and finishing none.

*The Page of Wands* is reliable, assiduous and studious. He is loyal, if stoical. Reversed, however, he is dull, unimaginative and stuck in his ways. When he shows up, he promises good news about a young relative or friend and a communication that will contain good news.

*The King of Cups* is an approachable man – someone you can trust and respect and who always puts people first and believes that people are innately good. But he can be filled with anger and become excessively flirtatious when the card is reversed.

*The Queen of Cups* represents fertility. She is creative, intuitive and peace-loving, at ease and in tune with others: the sort of woman who often has the answers to matters that are causing concern. She can be aloof, though, even when upright. Reversed she is emotionally possessive and squanders her emotions in looking for ideal, not real friendships.

*The Knight of Cups* is the Sir Galahad of the pack, the knight in shining armour, offering spice to life, sentiment and romance and seeking the Holy Grail of Perfection. But he is a shallow young man to whom consistency is a foreign word.

*The Page of Cups* has his head in the clouds – a kind, generous dreamer who is easily hurt and feels other people's pain, too, as well as being sensitive to their needs. When he is reversed, he becomes unworldly and oversensitive to criticism.

*The King of Pentacles* is a practical, honest and generous man who has made a success of his life, working hard for his family, which is the centre of his life. You may care to listen to what he says. But reversed, he becomes materialistic, over-cautious and obsessed with detail and should be ignored.

*The Queen of Pentacles* is hard-working and practical, particularly when it comes to money. She cares for the sick and those in need, not by offering advice, but by coming up with real solutions. Reversed she is prone to martyrdom, obsessed with order and overkeen to take over.

*The Knight of Pentacles* is a stable character, counselling caution where others rush in. He has a deeply felt respect for the world. He will never try anything unless he is absolutely sure it will work. Reversed, he lacks vision and is reluctant to explore the world beyond his own back door.

*The Page of Pentacles* is the sort of young man you can always depend on – reliable and hard working, loyal and steady. Reversed he becomes sadly unimaginative and something of a dullard.

*The King of Swords* may seem rigid and unsympathetic, but he has a strong sense of responsibility and has achieved success through his use of logic and clear thinking. When he is reversed, he is a cold, cruel calculating pedant.

*The Queen of Swords* is loving and kind, but you have to dig deep beneath the surface to find these qualities, because on the surface she seems critical and disappointed, embittered by life experiences and sorrows. She is a powerful ally, especially in times of adversity.

*The Knight of Swords* is a derring-do character, challenging injustice wherever he sees it and showing courage against the most alarming odds. A staunch and true friend. Reversed he becomes obsessive and over-willing to sacrifice others for the causes he believes in.

*The Page of Swords* is a clever and humorous young person, watchful and, despite youth, aware of injustice and of life's limitations. Reversed, beware of his deviousness with a disregard for other's feelings.

# The complementary Arcanas

You can use all the cards in the pack to do a reading or you can use just the Major Arcana or the Minor. Use the Major cards alone to interpret their messages regarding your soul's journey through life, and the archetypal aspects of your character. A Minor reading shows how you are affected by daily issues such as home, health, family and work. Using both Arcanas gives an in-depth perspective and an overall view of what is happening in your life.

It is even possible to do a simple reading using just the court cards. Shuffle them and lay them face down in a circle. Select four cards, surrendering to your instincts, and place them in a pile. Dealing from the top, place a card, face down, nearest to you. Read this, before placing the second card directly above the first. Repeat the process, until you have four cards in a vertical line.

The first card, the one nearest you, is who you are now. The one above is who will help you. The third card tells who will oppose you. And the fourth is who you will become.

The Tarot is a complex system of divination, its meanings subtle but deep. On a superficial level it is just another form of 'fortune telling', but the cards have a deeper significance offering insights into the forces at work both in your life and within your innermost self.

You have to work hard to get the most out of the Tarot, but remember that words are no substitute for experience and being taught by others is no substitute for using your own instincts. Surrender to them and you will be richly rewarded.

# Fortune telling with playing cards

'Ordinary' playing cards are derived from the Minor Arcana and court cards of the Tarot. The first cards to arrive in Britain came from France five hundred years ago, probably from the city of Rouen, and the design of the cards is still based on a pattern used all those years ago. The court cards still show figures wearing clothes that date back to the fourteenth century. According to legend these costumes derive from the pack designed by Odette, the mistress of Charles VI of France, having been given a pack by gypsies who brought them from the East.

The suitmarks – spades, hearts, diamonds and clubs – are also French, although we have given them English names. Since they were introduced to Britain, what we now call 'the English pattern' has spread to the United States and other English-speaking countries. In other parts of the world, playing cards have developed differently. France uses cards that are slightly different from ours, although the four suits remain the same; Italy, Spain, Germany and Switzerland have packs that are all quite different. Clubs becomes Acorns in Germany and Switzerland and Swords in Italy and Spain. Diamonds are Bells in Germany and Switzerland and Coins in Italy and Spain. Spades are Flowers in Switzerland, Leaves in Germany and Batons in Spain and Italy. And Hearts are Shields in the Swiss pack, Hearts in the German one and Cups in the other two.

What is constant is that in these, and in all other countries where cards are played, they are used to divine the future – and, being descended from the Tarot, probably always have been. The same legend that credits Odette with designing the court cards also has it that she and her royal lover were shown the oracular power of the cards by a gypsy who not only correctly foretold events but also whispered secrets that were only known to the King and his paramour. Another charming legend has it that Napoleon used the power of the pack to divine the right moment to mount his campaign to win the heart of Josephine Beauharnais. We don't know what spread he used, but we do know he captured her affections and held them until politics demanded that he divorce her in favour of an Austrian princess.

As with the Tarot, the cards may be read for you or for
anyone else and can be used to answer a simple question
or to give a more in-depth reading.

Tradition has it that cards that are to be used for
divinatory purposes should be used for no other purpose
and should be wrapped in black silk when not in use.
Some people also believe that if the cards are kept on a
high shelf, this raises what the cards say to a level that is
above worldliness.

If the reading is for someone else, shuffle the pack first
and then give it to the querent (some say left hand to left
hand, but as usual let instinct be your guide) to be shuffled
or mixed again.

The pack is now cut three times by the querent, again
with the left hand, and the cards spread out face down,
either in an overlapping row or a circle. (The reason for
using the left hand is that it is believed to have symbolic
access to the right side of the brain, the side that controls
intuition.) The cards to be read are then selected at
random, and put in the spread.

Any of the spreads that we looked at earlier can be
used when using ordinary cards to divine the future.
Among others is the mystical seven spread that reinforces
the magical powers of the circle with the six-pointed star
known as Solomon's Seal, believed by medieval alchemists
to be especially powerful.

After the cards have been shuffled or mixed, seven
cards are selected from an overlapping circle of cards or
from the complete pack – in either case face down.

Beginning at twelve o'clock lay the first six cards, still
face down on the six points of the Seal, working clockwise.
The seventh card should be placed in the centre.

The first six cards are now turned over, in the order
in which they were placed in the spread before the
reading is started. Look at these cards. Does any one

suit predominate? Or is one notable by its absence? This can be as significant as the cards themselves. An abundance of clubs for example may indicate that career matters are to the fore. Similarly if the same card from each suit appears, this will also be significant. Four of the same number indicates a heightened result; three indicate that different forces are acting in harmony; and two of the same number can foretell conflicts of interest, reconciliation or maybe a new connection, depending on the suits.

Use your instinct to read the six cards in the order in which they were dealt, before turning over the card in the centre of the circle to reveal what is about to happen.

Another method is, once the cards have been shuffled by both reader and querent, to spread the cards out, face down, into a semicircle. Ask the questioner to select thirteen cards and put the rest of the cards to one side. Take the baker's dozen, turn them over one by one and read what your instinct and experience tell you, remembering that the card preceding and the card following will probably have some sort of connection.

This done, marry the thirteen cards with the rest of the pack. From now on, only the reader must shuffle or mix the cards. Spread the cards out, face down, in a semicircle and ask the querent to select any five cards. Turn them over one by one, explaining the significance of each one, and again remembering the influence of the card before and the card that follows.

Now put these five cards back in the pack and again shuffle them well. Ask the questioner to cut the pack into three, turn up each set and read the top three cards in each one, again remembering the way in which they temper each other.

Now, with all the cards face down, shuffle the pack one last time, and ask the querent to cut the pack in half.

Turn each half face up – the cards that reveal themselves represent the final outcome of most of the querent's hopes and wishes, the problems they will encounter and the answers that will help them to overcome these.

# The meaning of the cards

Because, in many cases, the position of the cards can change their significance, their individual and relative meanings can often be widely different. What follows can only be general. But experience shows that even so, this can be surprisingly accurate. As in most card games, the Ace is highest in value and importance.

## Clubs

Clubs are linked with ambitions and achieving them successfully, with career matters, health, business partnerships, communication and expansion. The suit also has strong connections with older, mature people.

The *Ace* signifies a new beginning and fresh ambitions. New ideas will flow from you and could lead to a new perspective on old problems or a chance to travel. It may indicate that the questioner yearns to be free from a restrictive situation. It can also say that illness lies ahead: if followed by a heart card it will afflict someone in the immediate family.

The *King* combines success and ambition, innovation and communication skills. But such a man can be impatient and insensitive to the needs of others. In matters of principle he is uncompromising. His appearance often presages that a dark, friendly man will lend a helping hand just when it is most needed.

The *Queen* is dark, gentle and pleasing. A good organizer with the energy who embodies the old saying, 'If you want something done, ask a busy woman.' She is tactful and can usually get what she wants without stepping on too many toes. But she can use up her energy and become overtired. She suggests that such a person will offer help. Trust her.

The *Jack* rushes from one activity to another with all the energy of youth. He is sincere but impetuous, prone to giving up if things don't go well. That said, he can become over-absorbed in a project when it is going smoothly. He foretells the appearance of a dark young man who is confused about something. It will be to the querent's advantage if they try to make him feel at ease.

The *Ten* says that a long-term goal is about to be realized and that it may involve a change of direction and the chance to learn new skills. Whoever draws this card can look to the future confident that personal happiness is certain. It can also suggest a legacy from an unexpected source, but also the loss of a good friend's company.

The *Nine* reflects overwhelming responsibilities leading to self-doubt and loss of confidence. So now is the time to delegate and press on with core matters confidently and with conviction. It says that if a friend offers advice, consider it very, very carefully before acting on it. In the longer term, it suggests that widowhood will come but not until old age has arrived.

The *Eight* says that now is the time to grab sudden opportunities that show themselves. This could be the time to strike out on your own because you are enjoying or are about to experience an upsurge in energy. It could also be that an invitation is about to wing its way towards you: think twice before accepting it. It also warns against indulging in speculation and to beware of a greedy individual.

The *Seven* denotes personal success and satisfaction, but in achieving this, personal principles may have to be fought for. Happiness is on the horizon or just over it and will come with the achievement of a long-term goal. The card can also be a warning to beware of the opposite sex and that if you are asked to sign an important document, to take legal advice if you have any doubts about it.

The *Six* forecasts a period of calm on the work front, the perfect time to take a break and recharge your batteries. Use this time to network and establish contacts for new ventures. If you have been under the weather, you will probably have noticed that you are feeling better, something that is set to continue. If someone new is introduced into your circle, welcome them with open arms and you will make a friend for life.

The *Five* often turns up to tell the querent that this is the time to argue their case, especially regarding matters outside the home. Tiredness and carelessness brought about by the stress of being involved in other people's problems may cause accidents to happen and ill-health could be about to lay you low. Rivals could well be particularly uncommunicative and if you receive a letter from one, read between the lines, especially if it comes from abroad. It's not all bad news, though. The Five indicates a good and happy marriage.

The *Four* tells you that it's time to move on, and shake off the yokes in which others have bound you. It's also a time when you have to win the trust of others, to establish clear communication even if in doing so you feel you are holding yourself back. It may also be that a friend lets you down about a promise made earlier. Before you let fly at them, find out why: there could be a very good reason for their change of heart.

The *Three* says that an opportunity to expand your horizons is about to present itself. If you have been putting off making decisions about travel, make them now. On the work front, extra commitments, new opportunities and the input you are expected to put into them will require all your energy. The card can also indicate that the querent will be married more than once and news that a young person is ill may be received. But it is not too serious.

The *Two* indicates a disappointment of some sort, but don't give in to the temptation to bottle things up. This could be the time to reflect on things, and it may herald a period when plans that involve others appear to be restrictive. The card also advises that the questioner needs to work to achieve a balance between work and health, and that, to succeed, a business relationship may have to be reassessed.

## Diamonds

Diamonds refer to practical matters – money, property in general and the home, animals and children. The suit reflects qualities of patience.

The *Ace* augurs new ventures of a practical or financial nature. It promises a flood of prosperity and perhaps a change of home. But the surge in prosperity that is in the air lessens if the card is followed by a spade.

The *King* is a reliable man on whom you can always depend and turn to for advice, the sort of person who ensures that your life runs as smoothly as possible. He is patient and affectionate, but when he does show this side of his character, he does so in deeds rather than words. The King promises a great deal of travel.

The *Queen* is a practical and organized woman, one often in a long-term relationship. She is good at solving problems, particularly other people's. She has the happy talent of making everyone feel at home. Get her on your side and she will stick by you through thick and thin. But every coin has two sides, and if the Queen appears hard-hearted she is not to be trusted.

The *Jack* is a practical person who has youth on his side. He always shows common sense and a helpful attitude to others. These attributes and the responsible way he handles money might make him seem wise beyond his years. Like the Queen he is supportive in good times and bad.

The *Ten* radiates success, either financial or domestic. But if money is about to change hands, make sure that you are in control of the situation. The card smiles upon new plans, including a new domestic commitment, which it ensures will be successful.

The *Nine* counsels independent thought and action. It recommends putting personal interests first and says that the way to success is through expanding the horizons and perhaps speculating a little. A new business will bloom, but there may be a deal of extra work involved in making sure that it is firmly rooted.

The *Eight* announces the discovery of a new skill, which might well boost the income. It also says that there may be an unexpected change in domestic and financial arrangements. Any restless feelings experienced now should be channelled into making tangible improvements to your life. A short journey with some sort of bonus at the end can also be presaged by this card.

The *Seven* brings harmony at home and to financial matters. It favours long-term plans and says, 'don't rely on common sense all the time; trust your intuition and trust your dreams'. New happiness could well come into your life courtesy of children or maybe animals. There's also the whiff of change in the air, perhaps in the form of a new job.

The *Six* stresses that if you receive any documents, remember that the Devil is in the detail. Avoid making too many commitments now and keep a cautious watch on your finances, for this is a time for conserving energies and reflecting on things rather than rushing into action. And if anything is going to take up more time than usual, it will be family matters. An unexpected gift could also be coming your way.

The *Five* may put temporary financial or practical obstacles in your path and these may make you feel isolated or detached from life. But don't give up, look for advice or a new source of help, and whatever you do don't abandon plans: modify them, building on them to move on to greater things. Be on guard lest you lose something of value when this card turns up, especially if it is followed by a spade card.

The *Four* puts limits on monetary and practical matters and makes you ask whether you should keep what you have, or take a chance with it. There may be difficult decisions to be made concerning the home or the family, especially children. And even if the problems you face concerning property and money seem insoluble, hang on in there: they're not. If you are approached by someone, especially a fair young man, and asked for a loan a day or two after this card appears, make sure that you know exactly what is involved.

The *Three* suggests that a recently embarked-on venture is built on solid foundations. It can also presage a birth in the family (the chances of this are increased many fold if the Ace turns up in the same spread). Extra commitments or responsibilities may seem something of a burden, but they will be worth it in the long term. A disappointment regarding a journey may be in the offing, especially if the card is followed by a club.

The *Two* says that a new venture will turn out to be built on firm foundations. Increased prosperity is on the cards, too, as well as the prospect of a change of address.

## Hearts

This suit is linked with love and emotions, relationships and intuitions, young people who have left their teenage years behind but have not reached forty and people, regardless of age, who are in love.

The *Ace* signifies that the querent is on the brink of a new friendship that could blossom into romance. It also says that while one chapter in the book in which the emotions are written may be about to close, the first words have been written in a new one, especially if a romance has just come to an end. If a sudden burst of intuition has just been or is experienced in the near future, trust it.

The *King* indicates a charismatic, older man who has the happy knack of making people he talks to feel that they are the only people in the whole world who really matter. When he is faithful, he is a tender-hearted romantic, but he can wear his heart on his sleeve, so beware. The King can also represent an altruistic type who, in accepting the burden for his share of the world's troubles, puts his personal emotions on the sidelines.

The *Queen* is an older woman who is established in a long-term relationship. She is a caring, nurturing person who is always willing to lend an ear to those with troubles to share. And therein lies her weakness. She has a tendency to sentimentality and is prone to letting herself be so flooded by the sorrows and emotional needs of others that she drowns her own identity. And her willingness to be the emotional blotting paper of others may mean that they never reach full emotional independence.

The *Jack* is the one who, more than any other, loves being in love – but for sentiment's sake. The card indicates a young person, or an older, emotionally vulnerable, incurable romantic who is seeking perfection. He can also stand for the querent's best friend.

The *Ten* indicates that when emotional happiness and fulfilment come it will be through others. It is a lovely card to turn up, indicating someone who gives emotionally with every ounce of their being and who gets tremendous satisfaction from caring. It is a card of happy marriage blessed with many children and long-term, permanent relationships. The ten of hearts alters the negativity of any adjacent bad card and makes positive ones even more so.

The *Nine*, sometimes known as the card of the heart's desire or the wish card, is one of self-confidence and emotional independence. It talks of happiness in love or that a new venture of some kind will bring a rise in esteem and a boost to the finances.

The *Eight* warns to beware of jealousy, of emotional blackmail and says that a strong emotional attachment could be potentially destructive and should be brought to an end. But it can mean good news, signifying a holiday or break with a loved one or a friend whose company will bring great pleasure, and that one relationship is about to enter a new phase.

The *Seven* tells you to trust your instincts and intuition, to listen to what your dreams are saying to you. It says that you are in tune spiritually with those close to you and that friends and colleagues are in a mood of happy co-operation. Conversely, depending on the other cards in the spread, it can warn you to be on your guard lest someone you thought was a friend turns out to be fickle and false.

The *Six* presages a time of harmony in friendship and harmony in love. Good friends will bring a positive influence to bear on your life and if there have been rifts brought about by differences in attitude, particularly with

older people, accept that differences in the way we look
at life need not be a barrier to friendship. The six of hearts
can also herald good news about a child's endeavours
paying dividends.

The *Five* foretells that misunderstandings and jealousy,
albeit unfounded, may be about to cloud the horizon, but
that if you communicate from the heart, then they won't
last for long. It says that while passion is all very well it
should not rule our lives. Not only that, it counsels that it
is better to see a relationship for what it is and accept it for
that, rather than search for the Holy Grail. It also says that
an invitation with a romantic link may make you think
twice but you can accept it.

The *Four* is a card that gives voice to the possibility of some
sort of emotional choice having to be made, especially
if there are any doubts about the strength of another's
commitment. It is, therefore, a card that can indicate a
feeling of restlessness and dissatisfaction with the emotional
side of our lives. The card often appears in a spread
concerning a person with a deep love of art and music.

The *Three* revels in the rivalry that love or even simple
friendship (is there such a thing as simple friendship?) can
encourage. It can indicate an emotional tug o'war between
two rivals for your affections, and that the pressure,
emotional blackmail even, to which you may be subject
could herald a period of stress, which could be intensified
by the querent's imprudence.

The *Two* augurs well in the love stakes, indicating
that a love match is about to be made that could lead
to marriage. Friendships will deepen, long-standing
quarrels mend, bridges be built and two seemingly

unconnected aspects of life will come together in a totally unexpected way as long as care and attention are brought to bear.

## Spades

Perhaps the most challenging of the four suits, spades are associated with older people and with ageing in general. The suit is connected to the didactic, formal and traditional, to coping with challenges, especially those that can be seen as limiting in some way and to justice.

The *Ace* presages that a difficult time, perhaps involving some sort of sadness, is coming to an end and that a new day dawns as new challenges open new doors. The card also predicts an appreciation of a new form of learning. There is a bad side to this card, though, for it can foretell misfortune and malice. One well-known sage believes that when the Ace of Spades is facing up, news of a birth is in the offing, and conversely when facing down, there's a death in the air.

The *King* is not just an authority figure, but a harsh, disapproving and pedantic perfectionist. He may have accumulated a vast store of knowledge in his journey through life, but this only serves to make him impatient of the mistakes other people make. If he has an Achilles heel, it is that rather than being seen as vulnerable, he appears only happy in his own company. His appearance may signify that a legal matter concerning a dark man may affect the querent.

The *Queen*, often known as the Queen of Sorrows is a critical, disapproving, mature woman – the office bitch, the neighbour with the malicious tongue, the music-hall mother-in-law from hell. Afraid of being alone, she becomes possessive of her family and friends, all of whom she will defend tooth and nail, for loyalty is her cardinal virtue. When the Queen turns up in a spread, the querent is being warned not to trust such a woman, even if appearances suggest that he should.

The *Jack* is young, or immature, with a hurtful tongue, which gives voice to his sarcastic wit, which those at whom it is not directed often find clever and very funny. But look below this sometimes malicious façade and you may find someone who has been hurt, which is probably the reason why he is cruel and distrustful.

The *Ten* – the card of disappointment – but temporary disappointment, for there are good times just around the corner. It can mean that events in some aspect of life have run their course and that a new beginning beckons, so look to the future with optimism. The ten often turns up when financial worries are to the fore, news of which may be brought by a third party.

The *Nine* says that no obstacle is insurmountable if it is approached with courage and determination. You may think you know a little, but you know more than you may think, so if you fear failure and rejection, there's no need. Be confident and remember that victory has to be fought for, not thought about.

The *Eight* indicates some form of change, but only if you can cut your ties with yesterday and view the future with confidence. Don't be afraid to give voice to your fears, for if you do you will see that the future has many more possibilities than you thought possible, thanks to new contacts and previously unexplored avenues. The eight can also herald a time when frustration will turn to anger and anger to tears.

The *Seven* says that if logic fails and expert opinion is against you, intuition is there to be your friend. Use it. Make the most of any advantages you have over others, even if, in doing so, there could be conflict: remember, you have right on your side.

The *Six* signifies unexpected help from officials, which ushers in a period of unexpected calm after an unsettling time when self-doubt may have dominated thinking and actions. The card also changes things where a relationship that has been going through a bad patch is concerned, seeing it sail into much calmer waters. But, depending on the other cards, the six of spades can also indicate that angry words with someone who is not related are threatened, and the words 'think before you speak' should be kept in mind.

The *Five* tells you to marshal your facts and be prepared to use them if you are to avoid the spiteful actions and dishonest dealings of others. The fact that other people may not have the same high standards as the querent should not allow disillusionment to set in and cause long-laid plans to be abandoned. But seeing these through to successful completion may mean that ambition succeeds at the cost of openness.

The *Four* says that any inner fears that are based on past disappointments, perhaps betrayal, may strew limitations and obstacles in the path of achieving ambitions. Life's little injustices may cut deep, but the wounds are soon healed, so move forward even though doing so means taking losses that seem unfair.

The *Three* advises that if reason is brought to bear, rivalry and malice can be swept to one side. It says that challenges should be accepted and obstacles will be overcome even if doing so costs time and effort. And things that appear trifling now will gain significance in the future.

The *Two* is a card that indicates that a choice between unappealing alternatives may have to be made. Logic is called for, especially if the choice concerns conflict between two acquaintances or perhaps two distinct aspects of life. Or it could be having to choose which of two pieces of information to believe. The card can also warn to beware lest there's an unfortunate accident, that there may be a period of separation from a loved one and that spiteful gossip may hit home.

# It's in your cups

Reading the tea leaves – tasseography – is often associated with Romany folk or with women with 'the gift' rather than with mainstream divination. But it has a long and noble history, probably beginning not long after tea was first drunk, in China, perhaps as early as 3000BC. According to legend, the very first tea leaves came from Buddha, who cut off his eyelids to prevent himself from falling asleep while he was meditating. These eyelids fell to earth and from them a tea bush grew!

True or not, what we do know for a fact is that tea-drinking spread throughout the Orient and India, from whence Romany folk brought it, and the associated tea-leaf divination, to Europe.

Tea was an expensive luxury in Britain (so expensive that it was kept under lock and key in tea caddies) until the nineteenth century when large quantities were imported from India and Ceylon (present-day Sri Lanka), and so tasseography was a rare skill. But the art of divination from the dregs was practised long before that. The Ancient Greeks probably studied the dregs of the wine glasses for clues to what the future held, and whenever herbal remedies were brewed to give to the sick, what remained in the cup would be peered at by a spey wife (a Scottish expression for a woman who has divinatory skills).

Every one who reads tea leaves has their own rituals and often their own interpretations of what they see. Some people pour the tea into a cup through a strainer and either use what is there to peer into the future, or do so in association with the leaves left in the cup after it has been drunk.

Best is a good, traditional tea, the leaves of which are separate and firm, such as Earl Grey or Darjeeling. Make the tea as you usually do – most people swirl boiling water round the pot to warm it before putting the tea in – one spoon per person and 'one for the pot' is a steadfast recipe for a good brew.

As the tea is brewing (three to four minutes is usually enough) ask whoever has questions to ask to concentrate on them. It's not cheating to ask them what it is that concerns them. Pour the tea into plain white cups and enjoy drinking it – don't rush, just sip it as usual. If you want to continue concentrating, that's fine. If you want to enjoy a chat (a euphemism for a good gossip), that's all right, too, for one of the secrets of successful tea leaf reading is relaxation.

When the moment comes it's time to get down to the business in hand. As mentioned earlier, rituals vary from person to person. One well-tried and trusted method is for the querent to take the cup in their left hand and swirl it three times widdershins for a woman (clockwise for a man). The cup is then placed rim down on the saucer to drain away any tea that remains. The reader should then take the cup in their own left hand and interpret the patterns the leaves have made. Again, as with all other methods of divination, let instinct be your guide.

It's not just the leaves that are important – the position within the cup where the shapes form also influences things. For convenience the cup is mentally divided into four quarters.

The quarter nearest the handle represents the querent. Leaves that stick to the cup in this area are concerned with him or her, their home and those closest to them. Depending on the images, masses of leaves that stick to the cup here could suggest that the questioner is being overwhelmed by responsibility for family and close friends, or it can mean that home and personal life is particularly rich.

The side opposite the handle is concerned with strangers, acquaintances rather than friends, the workplace, travel and other matters away from home. A large concentration here suggests that these are the matters that concern the querent at the moment more than the family and the home.

To the left of the handle (from the seer's angle) is the area that stands for the past, with people moving out of the querent's ken. Unusually large areas here indicate that things unresolved in the past are having a bearing on the questioner's life. This is reinforced if there is an especially large concentration of leaves in this area, and if they are particularly dark.

The part of the cup to the reader's right is the area where leaves gathered represent upcoming events and people who are about to have an influence on the querent's life. No leaves here should not be taken as a bad omen, that there is no future: rather, that the questioner is more concerned with the present and the past than with what life holds in store.

As well as being divided into four quarters, the cup is also cut in two (metaphorically speaking) horizontally. Images close to the rim indicate the present – days and weeks – those clinging to the lower part of the cup indicate the more distant future – months and years.

According to Romany tradition a dry cup heralds good news: but if there is a trace of liquid remaining in the cup, there will be tears before the week is out. Also, according to the travelling folk, the rim of the cup equates with joy and happiness, the bottom with sorrow.

# An A – Z of shapes

Different symbols often mean different things to different readers. To one well-known tasseographer, an acorn indicates a pregnancy, a nearby initial giving a clue as to who will be so blessed! To another, the same symbol near the rim of the cup foretells financial success; in the middle it is equated with good health; and at the bottom it is an indication that both health and finances are due for a boost. A third reader sees the fruit of the oak tree as a general sign of health and plenty. What follows is a general guide to some of the symbols most commonly discerned in the cup.

*Aeroplanes* presage an unexpected journey that might be linked with a disappointment in some way. It may also mean new projects and a rise in status.

*Anchors* say that a journey will come to a successful end and that if the querent is at present having a bumpy ride through life, stability will soon be restored. At the top of the cup, an anchor can indicate a boost in business; if it's in the middle a voyage that boosts prosperity is indicated; and if it's near the bottom, social success is beckoning.

*Angels* herald good news.

*Ants* suggest industry and hard work, perhaps working with others to bring a project to a happy completion.

*Apples* promise a rosy future in business is ahead; and as they are regarded as symbols of fertility, they also represent good health.

*Arches* link the querent with marriage or long-term relationships. Someone regarded as an enemy may be about to extend the hand of friendship.

*Arrows* usually mean bad news. If the arrow is pointing towards the querent, he or she may be in danger of an attack of some kind; pointing away, he may find himself on the offensive. BUT, there is a school of thought that sees arrows as the bearers of good news in career and financial matters.

*Axes* may see the questioner having to chop away unpleasant difficulties.

*Babies* presage new interests.

*Baggage* – the sort you take on holiday – can mean the obvious. But it can also signify that the questioner is carrying about unnecessary emotional baggage that should be dumped as soon as possible.

*Bags* are a warning that a trap may be about to ensnare the querent.

*Balls* say that the querent will soon be bouncing back from current difficulties. Balls can also suggest that someone involved in sport will have a significant influence, probably bringing a changeable future.

*Balls and chains* are a sign that current commitments may be hard to shed, but that they need to be.

*Balloons* suggest that troubles may float in – but they will soon drift off again.

*Baskets* are a sign that can carry gifts with them. If full someone in or close to the family could have some news of a happily pregnant kind to impart. An empty basket, though, can mean that the questioner is giving too much of themselves to others, leaving his own emotional larder empty.

*Bears* bring with them a suggestion that travel to a foreign land is on the cards. A bear can also say that a strong ally will offer protection in a time of oncoming need, and that he or she will give you the strength you require to resolve a difficult situation.

*Bees* buzz with the news that change of some sort is in store for family or close friends.

*Bells* chime that marriage is in the air.

*Birds* sing that good news may soon be winging its way into the querent's life. If they are flying away from the handle, a departure could be round the corner, perhaps a fledgling is about to leave the nest. If they are winging their way towards the handle, a new opportunity is on the way.

*Boats* are an indication that some sort of important discovery is on the horizon. A boat also signifies a visit from a friend and flags a signal that soon a safe harbour will be reached.

*Books*, if open, suggest that startling revelations are waiting in the next chapter of life. An open book also says that to move ahead, a secret may need to be shared. It is also a sign that legal actions could follow, but that if they do they will come to a successful outcome. A closed book means that a delay of some sort will affect plans for the future.

*Boots* are a sign that caution is needed, according to some with the gift. To others a boot means achievement, and that if the querent is seeking protection for some reason, it will be theirs. But if the footwear is pointing away from the handle then a dismissal of some sort is in the offing. And if they are broken, then a failure looms.

*Bottles* suggest that illness may lie in store, but one on its own says that the querent's life will soon be bubbling over with pleasure. A full bottle is an encouraging sign to channel energy into a new challenge. An empty one is a sign of exhaustion and that health matters may soon be a cause for concern. A half-full one? It could be half-empty! And that's the difference between an optimist and a pessimist.

*Boxes*, when open, say that any romantic problems afflicting the questioner will soon vanish. Closed they mean that a recent lack of determination will vanish.

*Branches*, if in leaf, herald a birth. If bare, then disappointment of some sort looms.

*Bridges* present an opportunity for success that will soon cross the querent's path.

*Brooms* sweep change into life, suggesting that a good clear-out (both physically and emotionally) might be no bad thing.

*Buildings* suggest that a change of address may be just around the corner.

*Butterflies* say that innocent pleasures are about to flutter through the questioner's life, offering regeneration, and encouraging a carefree attitude pays dividends.

*Cages* are a sign that something is holding the questioner back, but they are also a sign of encouragement in that they say that the time will soon be when shackles can be shrugged off and it is time to move ahead.

*Cannons* see Guns.

*Castles* denote that circumstances are about to improve, especially if the questioner harbours a desire for luxury and pampering. They can also say that outside events affecting people who are not members of the immediate family are interfering with domestic happiness.

*Cats* bring treachery into view when they appear in the tea leaves, something that is reinforced if the feline back is arched.

*Chains* are a sign that links with other people will strengthen the sense of purpose.

*Cherries* mean that a victory of some sort is there for the taking.

*Chessmen* say that a short-term project should be put to one side, and that it is time to plan for the long-term if looming troubles are to be overcome. They also indicate that people are manoeuvring themselves into position for some oncoming conflict, and that it is time for the querent to follow their example.

*Cliffs* warn that the querent may be about to walk into a dangerous situation. But they can also suggest that the time has come to cast convention aside and live a little dangerously.

*Clouds* darken the bright skies of life with all sorts of doubts, but they should clear – eventually.

*Clover* is always regarded as a lucky symbol in reality, and it retains its fortunate connotations in the teacup, heralding as it does, prosperity in the offing.

*Coffins* signify if not death, then a loss of some kind.

*Coins* are a sign that money will soon cascade into the coffers.

*Cows* moo of prosperity and tranquil times ahead. Enjoy them while they last – the herd may soon move on to pastures new.

*Crowns* say that honours are about to rain down on the questioner; not just honours, but maybe a legacy along with the chances of a dream coming true.

*Daffodils* are a welcome harbinger not just of spring, but of wealth waiting just around the corner.

*Daggers* warn of danger, especially if impetuous actions are taken. They can also suggest that a sudden shock could be in store, one brought about by the plotting of enemies.

*Dice* are a sign that now is the time to take a risk and wait for the good times to roll in.

*Dogs,* being famed for their qualities of friendship and loyalty, when seen in the teacup say that good friends are coming the querent's way, especially if they seem to be running towards the handle.

*Donkeys* are a sign that says, 'Be patient and things will work out.'

*Doors* offer a potentially exciting step into the unknown that can be taken with confidence if the door is open, but not if the door is closed as the passage floor on the other side of the door is not yet ready to be trodden upon.

*Dots*, as well as speaking of money-making opportunities, also underline the meaning of any nearby symbol.

*Ducks* brings with them the chance perhaps to travel by water and of opportunity swimming in from abroad. Ducks can also say that if the querent has been searching to find his natural role in life, the search may soon be over.

*Drums* have quarrels and disagreements, scandal and gossip in their beat, and to see them in the teacup is a call to action.

*Ears* are a sign that the questioner should be on the alert because malicious rumours are being spread about him: or if they are not already, they soon will be.

*Eggs* signify an increase of some kind, perhaps springing from a new project.

*Eggtimers* say that if the querent is faced with completing a task of some sort, time may be running out.

*Elephants* are a good thing to see, signifying wisdom and a success, maybe thanks to the efforts of a trustworthy friend.

*Envelopes* bring with them news of some kind in the cup just as the letters they contain do in life – the main difference being that in the cup, they always mean some kind of good news.

*Eyes* are a warning to act carefully over the coming weeks.

*Faces,* when they are smiling, are a sign of happiness: but when frowning they say that opposition will soon stand in the way of any progress in the querent's life.

*Fans* herald flirtation, maybe leading to some sort of indiscretion.

*Feathers* are a sign that indiscretion and instability will upset the questioner in some way – but not too seriously.

*Feet* suggest that an important decision will have to be made in the near future and that if it is to lead to success, then the querent will have to act quickly. Feet also say that if he is to find success, he may have to look way beyond his own backyard to find it.

*Fences* – a warning that limitations are about to be imposed that will restrict the querent's options, perhaps because someone is being overprotective.

*Fingers* – when pointing to another sign, this emphasizes the second sign's meaning.

*Fingernails* point towards unfair accusations being made.

*Fish* bring with them some sort of good fortune, often the result of lucky speculation. They can also indicate that foreign travel is on the horizon.

*Flags* bring with them a warning of danger in the air, and suggest that to overcome it the querent will need to rally resources and act courageously.

*Flies* bring little domestic irritations, nothing serious, just constantly irksome things that will annoy the querent for some time to come.

*Flowers*, either a single bloom or a lovely bunch, presage a celebration of some sort. Flowers also signify that the questioner will be showered with small kindnesses that will make life worth living. One bloom can mean that love is about to appear, several that if the questioner is about to face an interview, there is nothing to worry about. If the flowers take the form of a garland, then recognition and promotion lie ahead.

*Forks* are a warning to beware flattery and false friends.

*Fountains* say that success lies in store for the querent. They also indicate that he or she is more interested in sexual passion than romantic love.

*Foxes* signify sagacity and foresight. They tell the querent that if she cannot achieve her aims by using persuasion, there is nothing wrong with subtlety or even stealth, but not at the expense of honesty.

*Frogs* are an indication that the questioner has the happy knack of fitting in no matter where he is. Frogs can also presage some sort of change, perhaps a change of address.

*Fruit* is a sign of prosperous times in store (see also Apples and Grapes).

*Gallows* warn that a loss is about to hit: it might be a financial one, or it could be that someone who was a good friend is about to be crossed off the querent's Christmas-card list. They can also suggest that he or she is feeling locked in a potentially dangerous situation from which he or she can see no means of escape – but desperately wants to find one. Conversely, if the questioner is not in the best of health, gallows are a sign of an upturn.

*Gates* can be good or bad, depending on whether they are open or closed. When open, prosperity and happiness lie ahead. But when barring the way ahead then they should be taken as a warning to be on guard against a loss of some kind, financial maybe or perhaps a valued possession is about to take wing.

*Geese* are not the most common of birds seen in the teacup, but if one or more is recognized, take it as a signal to heed any warnings that are issued in the near future. Doing so will save a situation: ignore them at your peril.

*Giants* foretell that a person with a magnetic and dominant personality is about to loom into view. Giants also suggest that huge strides will be made on the career front.

*Grapes* presage prosperity, a sign to squeeze every ounce of opportunity from chances that are about to present themselves. They are a sign of good health and an augury that this is the time to indulge yourself and give yourself a chance to make your dreams come true.

*Grass* suggests that something, an inner restlessness perhaps, is about to cause discontent, often with something that has to do with a long-term, but still developing situation with which the querent is involved.

*Guitars* presage great harmonious riffs, perhaps leading to romance. But they can also indicate a vain nature and a tendency to being irritable with those whom the querent considers to be of inferior talent.

*Guns* say that if other people's inertia has been harnessing progress, then now is the time to cut the ties that bind. Guns are also a warning that unless properly channelled, an outburst of aggression may have unfortunate results.

*Hammocks*, with their associations with long summer days spent snoozing, suspended between two trees, suggest an unconventional nature and perhaps a desire to opt out of responsibilities and take things easy.

*Hands* that are open and outstretched say that a new friendship is about to be forged – and that it will be mutually beneficial. If they are closed, though, someone is about to act in a very mean way, which is quite out of character.

*Hats* are a signal that change is the air, perhaps in the shape of a new job. Headgear can also herald the arrival of an unexpected visitor (Romany folk believe that it will be an old rival making an unexpected reappearance) or that an invitation to a formal occasion may turn up in the post.

*Heads* offer a hint to be on the lookout for new opportunities that could result in a promotion to a new position of authority.

*Hearts* whisper that a new friendship is around the corner, indeed it could already have presented itself: and it could be one that might lead to romance and, who knows, marriage. Hearts also indicate that a family situation is developing that will need to be handled with tremendous tact and sensitivity if it is not to end in a rift.

*Hens* cluck that an older person, probably a motherly type, will come to have an increasing influence in the querent's life, but that her over-fussiness will become more and more irritating.

*Hills* should be taken as a warning that the path ahead may become blocked, but the problems will be little ones and easily overcome and when they are, long-term ambitions will be achieved. If they seem to be shrouded in mist, take this as an indication of uncertainty over which of the mutually exclusive options that present themselves should be taken.

*Horns* are a welcome sign, cornucopias that will bring with them an abundance of happiness and peace.

*Horses* bring news of a lover, especially if just the head is seen. They are also a sign of good news generally. If they are at full stretch, galloping across the cup, they indicate that it may be time to saddle up and get travelling. If they are seen harnessed to a cart then they signify that a change of job or address is beckoning – a very advantageous one if the cart is full.

*Horseshoes* herald the same good luck in the cup as they did in the days when one found in a lane or byway was hung up above the front door to encourage good fortune.

*Houses* can indicate that there is nothing to fear in the days immediately ahead, for they bring security with them. But they can also say that domestic matters are about to take up an increasing amount of time.

*Icebergs* are a sign that someone the querent knows has hidden depths and that if they are not recognized there could be trouble in store.

*Igloos* say that seeking some sort of refuge from an emotional situation might be OK as long as it is recognized that doing so is a temporary measure and must not become permanent.

*Initials* represent the people for whom they stand and say that the signs closest refer to them rather than the querent.

*Ink spilt* in the cup represent doubts that must be clarified before the querent signs an important document, probably a legal one.

*Inkpots,* like ink, can have a legal aspect, indicating as they do that there are important legal or official matters to be communicated in writing.

*Insects* suggest little problems will irritate the querent – nothing serious, though, just thoroughly annoying, like a buzzing bluebottle that you keep swatting but never manage to get.

*Islands* have a duality of meanings. On the one hand, they can suggest that a holiday, to an exotic location perhaps, is coming up. On the other hand they can say that the querent is feeling increasingly isolated, probably in some matter on the work front.

*Jewels* say that someone is about to bestow an unexpected gift of a very generous nature on the querent.

*Jugs* are a sign that life is about to be brimful with good health if it is not so already. That's if they are full. Empty ones are a warning that money is being frittered away on unnecessary little luxuries.

*Kettles* whistle of domestic happiness – as long as they are near the handle. But if they are near the bottom of the cup, then the opposite holds true.

*Keys* are a sign of enlightenment and of new opportunities unless (and there is so often an 'unless' in reading the leaves) there are two of them at the bottom of the cup. If so, lock the doors and fasten the windows, for they warn of a burglary. They also signify an increasingly independent nature, perhaps of a child about to flee the nest.

*Kings* can warn that an older person may act in a high-handed manner that could be very upsetting. But it could be that he (or she) is acting out of a genuine desire to help and should be regarded as an ally – a very powerful one.

*Kites*, soaring around the cup, speak of lofty aspirations being successfully achieved.

*Knives* warn that a relationship is about to come to an end – the closer they are to the top of the cup, the closer that relationship will be. At the very top, then divorce is in the air. At the bottom, then lawsuits beckon – the closer to the bottom, the more acrimony will they bring in their wake. Anywhere else, they say, 'Beware of false friends!'

*Ladders* suggest that an advancement of some sort will present itself to the querent. It could be promotion at work, or it could be something more spiritual. They are also a sign that this is the time to set sights high.

*Leaves* are a welcome sign that good fortune is about to smile, bringing prosperity in its wake. Falling leaves hint that, come the autumn, some sort of natural turning point will be reached that will bring a surge of happiness.

*Letters*, the sort contained in envelopes, bring with them news from afar.

*Lines* have different meanings, depending on whether they are straight, slanting or curvy. Straight ones suggest progress in life, perhaps through a journey. Slanting lines speak of failure in business. And curved, wavy ones herald disappointments and uncertainty lying in wait.

*Lions* – the kings of the jungle signify powerful friends.

*Lizards* were scurrying around long before our ancestors descended from the trees, and as such are a sign to get in touch with primitive instincts and to trust them. They are also a warning to check all facts extremely carefully as the source may not be as reliable as it seems.

*Looms* see Spinning wheels.

*Loops* indicate that the path ahead is a crooked one; the end is in sight, but getting there is going to take forever as pointless disagreements and unwise decisions are going to make the journey seem interminable.

*Magnets* mean that a new interest will become increasingly important – and it could well be a romantic interest, meeting someone who is magnetically attractive and absolutely irresistible.

*Maps* can say that a desire to travel will soon be satisfied or that well-laid plans will give life a new destination. They can also signify that, after a long period of uncertainty, life gets back on an even keel.

*Maypoles*, once a common sight at spring fairs, indicate that new life is stirring after a period of dormancy. They also might herald news of a pregnancy or that a project started in the spring will come to a happy conclusion.

*Men* mean visitors, and if their arms are outstretched, then they are bearing gifts, so welcome them.

*Mermaids* sing that passion will lead to temptation and temptation to infidelity and infidelity to heartbreak.

*Mice*, peeking out from among the leaves, squeak of oncoming poverty, perhaps as the result of theft. They also say that this is not the time to be timid about anything and that if the initiative is taken, the benefits will be substantial. *Mirrors* might indicate that the querent is of a vain nature or that they feel that life is passing them by.

*Moles* suggest that secrets are in the air and that when they are revealed they will have a significant effect on the questioner's life. These 'little gentlemen in velvet waistcoats' can also point to the fact that a false friend is doing something that will undermine the querent in some way.

*The Moon* is one of the most often-seen symbols in the cup. If it is a full one (moon that is, not cup) then a love affair is in the offing. If it is a waxing moon, then new projects will prosper, and if it is waning then a decline in fortune is indicated. If it is partially obscured, then, sadly, depression is about to cloud the querent's life. And if it is surrounded by what look like little dots, tiny fragments of tealeaves, then marriage is in the air – but for money, rather than love.

*Monks* see Nuns.

*Mountains* can be a sign that obstacles, more serious ones than those indicated by hills, will appear and block the querent's view of the future. But they also stand for high ambitions that may or may not be achieved, depending on what else is in the cup.

*Nails* suggest that the querent is about to be hammered by malice, pain and injustice. That said, to get what is due, the querent will have to fight hard.

*Necklaces* suggest a secret admirer who, when he presents himself, may turn out to be the 'one'. A broken necklace, though, warns of a friendship that may be about to cool unless care is taken.

*Needles* have a trilogy of meanings. They can say that a quarrel is about to be settled to everyone's satisfaction. They might suggest that the best way to deal with jealous criticism is to brush it to one side. And lastly, if there's a needle in the cup an unsatisfactory situation is being tolerated in the hope that something will turn up to make things better.

*Nests* say that domestic matters are about to come to the fore and that someone is about to ask for the key to the door and become a visitor rather than a resident.

*Nets* can be taken as a sign that the questioner is feeling trapped or maybe worried about a new venture. They can also be taken to mean that something that has long been looked for is about to present itself.

*Numbers,* close to a leaf or leaves that indicate an upcoming event in the querent's life, tell the number of days that will elapse before that event will occur. Some numbers, though, have their own meanings. One signposts creativity, energy and new beginnings. Two is a sign of duality and rivalry, while three sometimes promises a betrothal. Four says that now is the time to accept that resources are limited and to work within them. Five is a sign that clear communication is needed when dealing with others. Six heralds peaceful and harmonious times. Seven points towards the unconscious world and says that it is now the time to put things into long-term perspective. Eight cautions the querent to follow convention, while nine suggests self-interest, as well as being a sign of a project being completed satisfactorily.

*Nuns* are indicative of a desire to go into retreat and withdraw from life for a while to ponder upon the best way to achieve a path that satisfies the material and the spiritual. The holy sisters can also represent wise friends who are always in the wings, waiting to help whenever called upon.

*Oars* say that the time has come to stop waiting for others to help and find a solution to whatever ails, perhaps by moving to a new house or new job.

*Octopuses* suggest that danger is about to entwine the querent in its tentacles, probably because he or she has overstretched available resources and taken on too much either in business or in personal life. On a happier note, they can also represent a multi-talented person who will be only too happy to oblige.

*Ostriches,* well known for burying their heads in the sand when danger threatens, say that the questioner shares that particular trait.

*Owls* warn that there's trouble perched on a nearby branch, ready to swoop down at any moment. The trouble in question could be brought about by gossip and scandal, or perhaps a failure of some sort. They also warn of neglected tasks. But they have a good meaning, too, signifying that a very wise person is standing by to help.

*Oysters* promise that the querent has hidden depths and talents that, if plumbed and used at the right time, will be of tremendous benefit.

*Padlocks,* when they are open offer the promise of the chance to get out of a difficult situation or to get out of an unwanted arrangement. When they are closed, then unspoken concerns about a job or a domestic matter are starting to bring their weight to bear.

*Palaces* see Castles.

*Palm trees* say that success will bring honour to the questioner, who may well be feeling a need to be cherished by family and friends. And being trees with exotic associations, they may be a sign that travel to an exotic place is on the horizon.

*Parachutes* announce that help is at hand if the querent is feeling vulnerable in any way. They can also mean that fear of failure or impending disaster can be dismissed for this is completely unfounded.

*Parrots* say that needless chatter and trivialities are clouding real issues. These talkative birds also warn that passing on gossip could have far-reaching and unfortunate results.

*Peacocks* promise that the querent's desire for a more luxurious lifestyle may be about to be fulfilled and if they are feeling proud at some recent achievement then quite right too. But they can also say that the vanity of friends poses a threat in some way.

*Pendulums* signify that the questioner needs to put some effort into restoring harmony with family, friends and colleagues. Another meaning is that there is a change of course on the cards, and a third is a warning not to take things at face value, to look below the surface to establish the reality of a situation.

*Pigs* might represent a generous, extremely hospitable friend, or they can warn that overindulgence could lead to ill health.

*Pigeons* may be an annoying fact of urban living but in tasseography they suggest that an unexpected communication will be received from far-off places, and that the bearer of the news is someone in whom the querent can have absolute confidence.

*Pipes* suggest that if careful thought is given to a problem, the solution will waft its way into the querent's mind.

*Pistols* warn of danger and that someone will use unpleasant methods to get their own way at the expense of the questioner.

*Precipices* see Cliffs.

*Purses* presage luck or gain, depending on whether they are open or shut. They tend to turn up frequently in the cups of people who have deep pockets and short arms.

*Pyramids* indicate a concern with healing and psychic powers. If they appear in the leaves of someone who the reader knows has a pressing problem, then the answer to it lies in the past not in the present.

*Question marks* suggest that hesitancy and caution should be the watchwords for the coming days.

*Rabbits* say that speed is of the essence, especially if there are enemies to confront. And with their association with being prolific breeders, they can also indicate that the querent is concerned with fertility in some way.

*Rainbows* signify that while some wishes may be about to be fulfilled, other, more unrealistic ones, may have to be put on hold.

*Rats* warn the querent to be on the lookout for a vindictive, deceitful person who has revenge in mind. On a brighter note, they might be saying that if open-handed methods have failed the querent, then now might be the time to try underhand ones!

*Ravens* suggest that a warning of some sort may be about to be issued, and that while it may be unwelcome, it would be extremely foolhardy to ignore it. And if the querent has been told something in confidence, it would also be unwise to break it.

*Rings,* if they are close to the top, mean that marriage is immediately around the corner. In the middle, then a proposal can be expected in the near, but not immediate future. If it is at the bottom then the engagement will be a long one, a very long one. The marriage that takes place, be it tomorrow, next year or several years down the line, will be a happy one if the ring is complete. If it is broken, then the marriage won't be happy or unhappy: the engagement will be broken off before the bride walks down the aisle.

*Roads* suggest that a new path is about to appear in the questioner's life. If they are straight, fine. But a fork suggests that a choice will have to be made – the wider the fork, the more important the choice.

*Rocks* strew the path ahead with obstacles and hazards. But all is not bad news, for they can be overcome without too much difficulty, and more positively, it may be that they can be used as building bricks or stepping stones to a better future with a little careful thought.

*Scales*, of the weighing rather than the fishy kind, are a sign of justice and judgement. In Ancient Egypt, after a death, the heart of the deceased was weighed against a feather to find out if they qualified for the afterlife. The oncoming judgement foretold by scales in the cup will not have such an eternal result – but it could be significant just the same. Balanced ones suggest a just, fair decision will bring benefits, unbalanced ones that the questioner will suffer through injustice.

*Scissors* presage domestic arguments and worse that they will become so bitter that separation is on the cards.

*Seesaws* can mean that mood swings will see the querent lightheaded with happiness one minute, down in the dumps the next. They can also indicate that the swings and roundabouts of life will make it hard to achieve a proper sense of balance.

*Sharks* say that some force may be required if attacks from an unexpected source are to be repelled with any chance of success.

*Shells* mean that good news is coming in with the tide. They also indicate intuitive wisdom and tell the questioner not only to listen to the inner voice that is called instinct, but to act on it.

*Ships* can say that an increase is on the horizon. They can also suggest that if the querent is worried about something he can cast any doubts overboard, because it will come to a successful conclusion.

*Snakes* have the well-known ability to shed their skins. Their appearance in the teacup suggests that it is time for the querent to, metaphorically speaking, get rid of current burdens and responsibilities and slide, regenerated, towards the future.

*Spiders* suggest to some readers that someone is spinning a web of subterfuge that will soon enmesh the questioner. To others it says that persistence will pay off financially.

*Spinning wheels* say two things. The good news is that they say that careful planning and consistent industry will bring good results. The bad news is that they can point to the fact that someone is plotting behind the scenes to the querent's detriment.

*Squares* were once seen as signs of some sort of restriction, but are now generally taken to mean that protection is there for the asking, if need be. They also say that if the querent uses the near future to lay down some careful long-term plans, it will lead to a boost of financial and material prospects.

*Squirrels*, as one might expect, carry the message that people who save for the future have less to worry about than spendthrifts who live for today and to hell with tomorrow.

*Stars* can shine with messages of hope, particularly where health matters are concerned. If they have five points, good fortune in general is there for the asking. But if the star is an eight-pointed one, accidents will cause reversals. If there are five stars a-twinkling in the cup, then success will come, but it will not bring any happiness. And seven stars say that grief may be about to strike.

*The Sun* says that the grey skies of disappointment will soon clear and happiness will beam down on the querent, bringing with it success and perhaps power. The Sun can mean, too, that the next summer will be an especially happy one, perhaps involving travel to a sunny destination.

*Swords* suggest that the querent should prepare himself for quarrels and disputes.

*Tables* indicate that social life is about to take a lively and positive upturn.

*Teapots* presage meetings – long, boring ones which will make the querent come to the widely held belief that any meeting of more than two people is a complete waste of time.

*Telescopes* say that the answers to present mysteries will soon be revealed, but that the answers lie outside the immediate environment.

*Tents* indicate a love of adventure, but one that could lead to an unsettled life.

*Tortoises* with their associations with longevity say that while success can be achieved, it will be a long time a-coming. They also indicate a love of tradition.

*Towers* can imply that the querent is feeling restricted in some way, unless they have steps, in which case they lead to a rise in status and a boost to the finances. A tower that is incomplete suggests that plans are not yet finished – and never will be.

*Trees* augur a growth in prosperity, brought about by long-held ambitions coming to happy fruition. Romany folk believe that if the tree is surrounded by smaller leaves, then these ambitions will be realized in the country, or at least they will be associated with it in some way.

*Triangles* can mean unexpected success or unexpected failure, depending on the way the triangle is pointing. Upwards is good; downwards bad, unless the querent realizes that there is still time to grab an opportunity that is just about to slip from his grasp.

*Tunnels* promise that present confusion and setbacks will soon be swept away, but only if the querent probes in the right places.

*Turtles* see Tortoises.

*Umbrellas* suggest that little annoyances are about to shower on the questioner. They also signify a need for shelter. If they are open, then that shelter will be found; if the umbrella is rolled up, then it will not be.

*Unicorns* offer the promise of magical insights that illumine the querent's life in some way. They also promise that unusual and unexpected opportunity is on the horizon.

*Vans* bring movement in their wake.

*Violins* see Guitars.

*Volcanoes* presage that an eruption of passion will soon sweep the querent off her feet. They often appear when the person whose leaves are being read is one who is seething with anger, but is determined not to let it show.

*Walking sticks* herald the arrival of a visitor.

*Waterfalls* bring prosperity with them.

*Weathervanes* point to inconsistent and indecisive friends. They warn the querent to be on the lookout for signs of change that, if recognized and acted on when the time is right, will lead to some benefit.

*Webs*, like their weaver, the spider, are a sign that deceit and subterfuge will have a significant bearing on the querent's life.

*Whales* promise the successful fulfilment of a big undertaking. They offer commercial and professional success, the latter especially if the querent is involved in one of the caring professions.

*Wheels*, if they are complete, say that good fortune is about to roll in. If they are near the rim of the cup, then the good fortune will come in the form of an unexpected legacy or win of some sort. But if the wheel is broken then disappointments loom.

*Windows* can mean good luck or bad luck depending on whether they are open or shut. They may offer new insights or a chance to explore new horizons, unless they are curtained, in which case they point to the fact that other people's narrow horizons are holding the querent back in some way.

# It's in the crystal

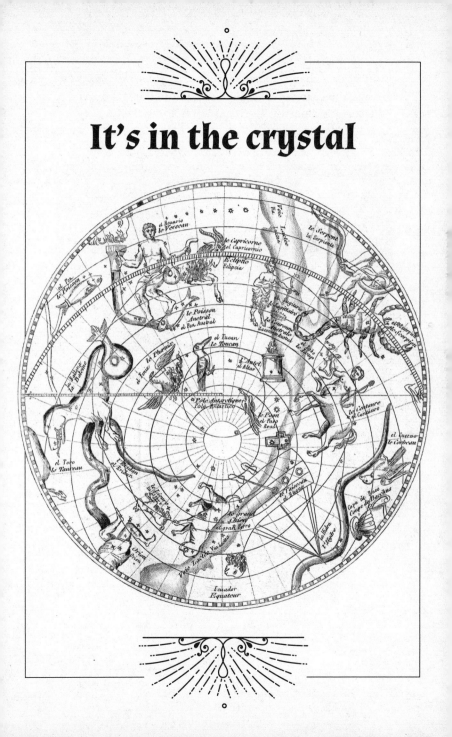

Think of divination and one of the images that probably comes to mind is that of an old crone peering into a crystal ball and making relevant what she sees in it to whichever question has been put to her. Not something to be taken seriously. Something that whiled away half an hour on a rainy afternoon during a traditional British seaside holiday in the days before cheap foreign travel whisked us off to sunnier destinations.

This image of the crystal gazer has probably done more to harm divination's reputation than any other, which is sad because crystal gazing has a long and honourable tradition as part of scrying – using crystals, mirrors, flames and water as a means to peer into the future.

Crystal gazing has its roots in prehistory, when the tribe member who was credited with the gift of seeing peered into a reflective surface to discern what lay round the corner. It was not necessarily a crystal: a stretch of calm, still water served the purpose just as well.

In slightly more modern times, Nostradamus, the famous seer whose prophesies continue to unfold many centuries after his death, would sit alone at night, gazing into a bowl of water held in a brass tripod and lit by a candle. In the mirror-like surface he saw his visions, that are still relevant in our lifetime. His English contemporary, Dr John Dee, whose divinatory talents were recognized by Queen Elizabeth I, used a shiny black obsidian mirror to help in his prophesying.

Traditionally, the ball used for crystal gazing should be a gift from someone with the talent, but nowadays they are easily available in a variety of crystals – clear or smoky quartz, beryl and obsidian are the most popular – and glass from specialist shops. Glass ones should be examined particularly closely for any blemishes or bubbles that could be distracting.

When buying one, the mood should be relaxed and receptive, an atmosphere encouraged in 'New Age' shops not just by the incense that is often burned there, but by the positive vibrations given off by staff and fellow customers. Handle several crystal balls, which are usually

about four inches (ten centimetres) in diameter. How do they fit in the hand? Are they perfectly plain spheres or do they have angles and planes within them. Most people find that when they go to buy their crystal ball, they keep returning to one, no matter how many they look at and handle. If this happens, that is the ball to buy.

To prepare the ball, wash it in a mild solution of vinegar and water, then polish it with a soft cloth. When it is not being used, the ball should be wrapped in a cloth to keep it out of direct sunlight, which affects sensitivity: and it should not be handled by anyone other than the user. Some gazers unwrap their crystal ball and put it in a moonlit place during a full Moon, which they believe enhances the crystal's power.

Crystals pick up vibrations when handled by other people. If someone else is to handle another's crystal ball, the hands must be cupped around it, and after use, the ball should either be washed in vinegar or water, or held under running water while visualizing it surrounded with bright, shining light. That done, it should be wrapped in silk or velvet until it is to be used again.

# How they work

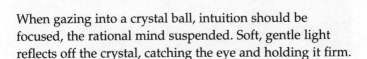

When gazing into a crystal ball, intuition should be focused, the rational mind suspended. Soft, gentle light reflects off the crystal, catching the eye and holding it firm.

It's not long before the eyes go slightly out of focus, the ball mists over and within the mist images start to form. These images are projections from the gazer's mind or inner crystal.

The room should be quiet, a place where the gazer will not be disturbed, and gently lit, in the words of one gazer,

'like daylight on a wet, cloudy day'. Some people use candlelight to achieve this, others swathe the lamps with a suitable (flame-retardant) cloth.

It is essential that the gazer is in a relaxed state of mind before beginning: some people can achieve this by deep breathing, others use visualizing techniques. As this is being achieved, the crystal should be held in the hands for a few moments to attune the ball to the gazer's vibrations. At the same time, questions can be framed, and safe solutions considered but not pondered on too deeply.

The ball is now placed on a black silk or velvet cloth, and perhaps partially surrounded with a black velvet or silk curtain or screen. Now stare at the crystal, until the eyes go out of focus, the mist forms and images appear within it. These images must not be forced: they should arise naturally. The images may appear in the ball or in the mind's eye. Even meaningless ones might have significance, so write everything down as it arises.

It takes time and concentration to gaze successfully into the crystal. But not too much time, and learning to concentrate properly is a talent that has many other applications, so it is well worth the effort. The first occasion should last no longer than ten minutes, gradually increasing the time of each session, at first to fifteen minutes, then twenty and so on, but no session should ever last longer than one hour. Time each session with a watch or clock positioned so that you can see its face, but will not be distracted by its ticking.

The presence of another person distracts concentration, at least at first. With experience comes the ability to answer the questions of others, as long as they are asked in a low, hushed voice.

Gazers often find that small glittering points of light appear in the mist, before the mist clears, and what has been described as an ocean of blue space appears, within which visions appear. These visions are sometimes symbolic, the meaning of the symbols being similar to those seen in a tea-leaf reading (see pages 79–110), or they may be scenic. Visions that appear in the background lie further ahead than those that are to the front, which denote the present or the immediate future.

When images come, no effort should be made to keep them there: they should be allowed to come and go, ebbing and flowing like the tide, with no attempt being made to control them.

# Crystal clear

Crystal-ball reading is not the only use to which crystals can be put for divination. An assortment of small crystals kept in a special bag can also be used. The simplest way is to shake the bag, and while focusing on the question to be asked, take out the first two or three that the fingers touch. As they are drawn, take a moment or two to see if the answer comes spontaneously to mind, before looking up the meaning of the crystals.

More complex questions can be answered and guidance for the future gained by using crystals in any suitable Tarot spread. And boards on to which crystals are thrown are available from specialist shops: the combination of the answers on the board and the sagacity of the crystals have satisfied countless users.

Generally, red, yellow, orange and sparkling-white (hot-coloured) stones contain a great deal of creative energy and indicate that some action is indicated with regard to the area with which the particular stone is associated. Green, blue, purple, pink and pearly white stones reflect spiritual desires, thoughts and emotions.

The associations of some of the more common crystals are as follows:

| Agate | Success in worldly matters |
|---|---|
| Amethyst | Shifts in consciousness and life changes |
| Black agate | Prosperity and courage |
| Blue lace agate | A need for healing |
| Red agate | Longevity and good health |
| Aventurine | Growth and expansion |
| Citrine | Wisdom in celestial matters |
| Diamond | Permanence |
| Emerald | Fertility |

| | |
|---|---|
| Jade | Immortality and perfection |
| Red jasper | Worldly affairs |
| Lapis lazuli | Favoured by the divine |
| Clear quartz | Self-healing and love |
| Ruby | Passion and power |
| Sapphire | Chastity and truth |
| Snowflake obsidian | Closure of a challenging time |
| Tiger's eye | The need to look beneath the surface |
| White quartz | Change of a profound nature |
| Unakite | Integration and composure |

# It's in the East

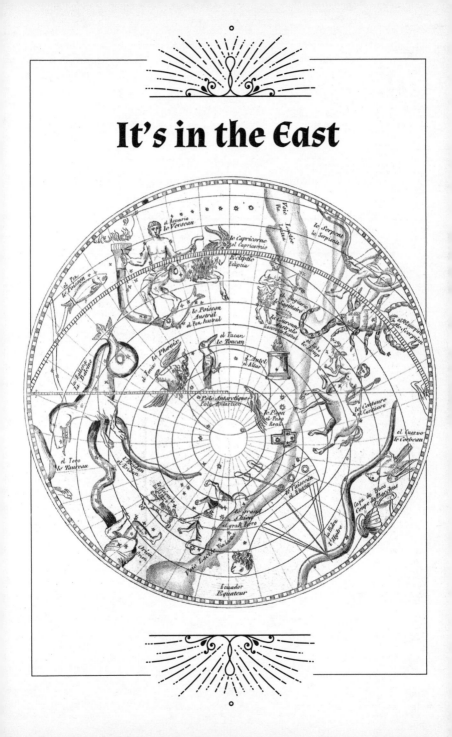

D ivination has been practised in Asia and the sub-continent of India for thousands of years, among some of the oldest civilizations in the world. And the practice continues today. Whereas the vast majority in the West pay scant attention to divination (although even the most cynical office workers will still borrow a colleague's tabloid newspaper and read their horoscope given half a chance), to millions of Chinese, astrology and the I Ching are a part of everyday life.

Whereas in Western astrology the Sun is central, Chinese astrologers look to the Moon for their inspiration. It is also influenced by, among other things, the Yin and the Yang, which poke their noses into every nook and cranny of Chinese life, and the four elements – Earth, Metal, Water and Fire. For example, a Fire Pig will have different characteristics from an Earth one, and a Water Rat will differ in several respects from a Metal Rat. Those seeking deeper knowledge could resort to the Internet or bookshops that specialise on the subject.

The table on pages 128-29 allows you to find out the lunar month in which you were born, which is crucial. You will see that in several years, one of the 'months' is almost twice the length of the others. This is because, although there are usually twelve lunar months each year, in 'leap years' there are thirteen. The names are seasonal in nature, and as the thirteenth month can occur in any season, the 'leap year' Moon is wedded to the Moon that precedes it, and those born on any date in the two-month period will share the same characteristics.

Thousands of years ago, the lives of the people who lived in the Yellow River Valley were subject to the same caprices of the heavens. They suffered floods and hailstorms, searing heat and devastating droughts – all of which were blamed on the movements of the stars and the planets. Some of the earliest recorded documents, dating from the period, correlate natural events to heavenly happenings. A flood may occur during an eclipse of the Moon, a drought may have hit when one or other of the planets could be seen in a particular place in the night sky and, as more events were recorded over the centuries, a vast body of knowledge about the cyclical nature of the universe was perceived.

Between 1500 and 1100BC the sages who recorded and pondered these events were thought to have divinatory powers, which saw them promoted to important positions of political power and influence. Being aware of the psychology of the ordinary people, these wise and ambitious men evolved a system that came eventually to be codified by philosophers such as Confucius and Lao-tze, who, to use a modern expression, put their own spin on things. They believed that if the known universe was influenced by recognizable cycles, then, by extension, so, too, was the nature of man. In a perfect world, the philosophers decreed, everyone would live for sixty years, which were divided by the five elements – wood, fire, earth, metal and water – resulting in twelve earthly branches, which would then evolve into twelve years each of which was assigned an animal. Each animal sign was then divided into lunar months, each of which, in turn, was ascribed specific attributes.

In Chinese astrology, the celestial bodies recorded in the second millennium BC, follow the same paths through the heavens today, continuing to influence us now as they did the men and women who toiled in the Yellow River Valley all those years ago.

As with many things Chinese – philosophy, medicine and astrology to mention but three – the basic concept that underlines ancient and modern thought and practice is Yin and Yang. They combine to make up the life force, Qi. In his famous book *Canon of Internal Medicine*, the Yellow Emperor claims that Yin and Yang constitute the basic principle that governs the entire universe, so it is not surprising that the years and months of the Chinese calendar have Yin and Yang aspects.

Yin is soft, dark, cold wet, its symbol a cloud-topped mountain. Yang is hard, bright, hot and dry, its symbol a sun at the centre of a crown of shining rays. In medicine, perfect health depends on achieving a balance between the two, as does perfect peace of mind. In Chinese astrology a Yin year can modify a Yang month and a Yang month a Yin year, something that has to be taken into account when using Chinese astrology to divine the future. Chinese astrology is based on years consisting of twelve months running in cycles of twelve years. Each twelve-month period is named after an animal which rules for a year before bowing to the next in the cycle. In the beginning these twelve cycles were simply referred to as the Twelve Branches, but slowly they were ascribed the characteristics of twelve animals. Why these twelve animals? One legend has it that Buddha invited all the beasts in the animal kingdom to celebrate the New Year with him, but only twelve arrived. The Buddha rewarded them by naming a year in their honour, the Rat having been the first to arrive was accorded the honour of having the first year in the cycle named after him: the last year was named after the last animal to arrive – the Pig. But there is no mention of these animals in the texts of the Han Dynasty, which was at its peak 500 years after the Buddha was alive. A more likely explanation is offered by those who believe the names were taken to China from Central Asia, perhaps as recently as AD800.

The twelve years are the Rat, the Ox, the Tiger, the Rabbit, the Dragon, the Snake, the Horse, the Ram, the Monkey, the Rooster, the Dog and the Pig. The Dragon is the only mythological beast in the menagerie and although it is a frightening beast to westerners, to the Chinese it is seen as a something of a benefactor. Each of the animals has a well-defined nature (not necessarily the same to the Chinese as it is to us) and people born in the year of a particular animal are thought to possesses its qualities.

Because the Chinese calendar is a combination of lunar and solar activity, the starting and finishing dates of each year vary from year to year. The Chinese New Year starts on the first day of the first Moon (see below), usually at the end of January or beginning of February. And whereas the western calendar adds an extra day to every fourth February to balance the monthly lunar cycle with the solar year, the Chinese add an extra month every seven years over a nineteen-year cycle. Therefore it is not possible to ascribe an exact western year to each of the signs in the Chinese horoscope. Someone born in 1995 may be a Dog if he was born between 1 January and 30 January that year or a Pig if he was born after that date.

Once the animal sign has been determined and general character traits identified, it is possible to refine things by taking into account the patterns suggested by the Mansions of the Moon, the romantic phrase the Chinese use to describe the twelve lunar divisions that make up each Chinese year.

Things are refined even further when the elements are taken into account. Each year is ascribed one of the five elements – Water, Fire, Earth, Metal and Wood – each of them straddling two years in succession before ceding power to the next in line. So, whereas all Rabbits share common attributes, they are not necessarily influenced by the same element. A Fire Dragon will be different in some way from an Earth one, and a Metal Monkey will have characteristics distinct from a Water Monkey.

Generally, Metal people tend to be rigid and do not give in easily. So, while all Oxen can be stubborn, a Metal Ox will be even more so. Metal people also insist on honesty and expect a great deal from their prospective partners. They may be remarkable for their strength of character, but, oh, how they like to dominate.

Water tends to lend creativity to a sign. It is a compassionate element and for those born under a sign whose subjects have a tendency to be caustic, if they have water as their element, this quality is diluted. Water also makes lovers yielding and easily influenced by their partners.

Wood and consideration go hand in hand, the element encouraging warmth, generosity and co-operation. Those with wood as their element will usually try hardest of all to see another's point of view.

Fire is the most dynamic of the five elements. When it is attached to a sign, the upside is that it encourages a sense of honour while the downside is that it can cause an inflexible temperament.

Earth people are hard workers, especially in making others see their point of view. They are patient, especially when they fall in love, and willing to wait for their affections to be returned, whereas other signs would give up and search elsewhere. Earth people can also be stubborn.

The first chart immediately below shows the Chinese Year from 1979–2018. The one below that will help to identify the moon month. By consulting this chart, someone born on 16 November 1985 will find that the tenth Moon started on November 12 and finished on December 12. They were, therefore, born in the tenth Moon.

# Chart of the years

| Year | From – To | Element | Animal |
|------|-----------|---------|--------|
| 1979 | 28 Jan 1979 – 15 Feb 1980 | Earth | Ram |
| 1980 | 16 Feb 1980 – 04 Feb 1981 | Metal | Monkey |
| 1981 | 05 Feb 1981 – 24 Jan 1982 | Metal | Rooster |
| 1982 | 25 Jan 1982 – 17 Feb 1983 | Water | Dog |
| 1983 | 13 Feb 1983 – 01 Feb 1984 | Water | Pig |
| 1984 | 02 Feb 1984 – 19 Feb 1985 | Wood | Rat |
| 1985 | 20 Feb 1985 – 08 Feb 1986 | Wood | Ox |
| 1986 | 09 Feb 1986 – 28 Jan 1987 | Fire | Tiger |
| 1987 | 29 Jan 1987 – 16 Feb 1988 | Fire | Rabbit |
| 1988 | 17 Feb 1988 – 05 Feb 1989 | Earth | Dragon |
| 1989 | 06 Feb 1989 – 26 Jan 1990 | Earth | Snake |
| 1990 | 27 Jan 1990 – 14 Feb 1991 | Metal | Horse |
| 1991 | 15 Feb 1991 – 03 Feb 1992 | Metal | Ram |
| 1992 | 04 Feb 1992 – 22 Jan 1993 | Water | Monkey |
| 1993 | 23 Feb 1993 – 09 Feb 1994 | Water | Rooster |
| 1994 | 10 Feb 1994 – 30 Jan 1995 | Wood | Dog |
| 1995 | 31 Jan 1995 – 18 Feb 1996 | Wood | Pig |
| 1996 | 19 Feb 1996 – 06 Feb 1997 | Fire | Rat |
| 1997 | 07 Feb 1997 – 27 Jan 1998 | Fire | Ox |
| 1998 | 28 Jan 1998 – 15 Feb 1999 | Earth | Tiger |
| 1999 | 16 Feb 1999 – 04 Feb 2000 | Earth | Rabbit |
| 2000 | 05 Feb 2000 – 23 Jan 2001 | Metal | Dragon |
| 2001 | 24 Jan 2001 – 11 Feb 2002 | Metal | Snake |
| 2002 | 12 Feb 2002 – 31 Jan 2003 | Water | Horse |
| 2003 | 01 Jan 2003 – 21 Jan 2004 | Water | Ram |
| 2004 | 22 Jan 2003 – 08 Feb 2005 | Wood | Monkey |
| 2005 | 09 Feb 2005 – 28 Jan 2006 | Wood | Rooster |
| 2006 | 29 Jan 2006 – 17 Feb 2007 | Fire | Dog |
| 2007 | 18 Feb 2007 – 06 Feb 2008 | Fire | Pig |
| 2008 | 07 Feb 2008 – 25 Jan 2009 | Earth | Rat |

| 2009 | 26 Jan 2009 – 13 Feb 2010 | Earth | Ox |
| 2010 | 14 Feb 2010 – 02 Feb 2011 | Metal | Tiger |
| 2011 | 03 Feb 2011 – 27 Jan 2012 | Metal | Rabbit |
| 2012 | 23 Jan 2012 – 09 Feb 2013 | Water | Dragon |
| 2013 | 10 Feb 2013 – 30 Jan 2014 | Water | Snake |
| 2014 | 30 Jan 2014 – 18 Feb 2015 | Wood | Horse |
| 2015 | 19 Feb 2015 – 07 Feb 2016 | Wood | Ram |
| 2016 | 08 Feb 2016 – 27 Jan 2017 | Fire | Monkey |
| 2017 | 28 Jan 2017 – 13 Feb 2018 | Fire | Rooster |

*If your birth year isn't shown on the chart, use this wheel
to find the animal for any birth year from 1935 to 2030.*

## Calculating the Moon Month

| Year | 1st | 2nd | 3rd | 4th | 5th | 6th | 7th | 8th | 9th | 10th | 11th | 12th |
|---|---|---|---|---|---|---|---|---|---|---|---|---|
| 1985 | 20.2 | 21.3 | 20.4 | 20.5 | 18.6 | 18.7 | 16.8 | 15.9 | 14.10 | 12.11 | 12.12 | 10.1* |
| 1986 | 9.2 | 10.3 | 9.4 | 8.5 | 7.6 | 7.7 | 6.8 | 4.9 | 4.10 | 2.11 | 2.12 | 31.12 |
| 1987 | 29.1 | 28.2 | 29.3 | 28.4 | 27.5 | 26.6 | 24.8 | 23.9 | 23.10 | 21.11 | 21.12 | 19.1* |
| 1988 | 17.2 | 18.3 | 16.4 | 16.5 | 14.6 | 14.7 | 12.8 | 11.9 | 11.10 | 9.11 | 9.12 | 8.1* |
| 1989 | 6.2 | 8.3 | 6.4 | 5.5 | 4.6 | 3.7 | 2.8 | 31.8 | 30.9 | 29.10 | 28.11 | 28.12 |
| 1990 | 26.1 | 25.2 | 27.3 | 25.4 | 24.5 | 22.6 | 20.8 | 19.9 | 18.10 | 17.11 | 17.12 | 16.1* |
| 1991 | 5.2 | 16.3 | 15.4 | 14.5 | 12.6 | 12.7 | 10.8 | 8.9 | 8.10 | 6.11 | 6.12 | 5.1* |
| 1992 | 4.2 | 4.3 | 3.4 | 3.5 | 1.6 | 30.6 | 30.7 | 28.8 | 26.9 | 26.10 | 24.11 | 24.12 |
| 1993 | 23.1 | 21.2 | 21.3 | 21.5 | 20.6 | 19.7 | 18.8 | 16.9 | 15.10 | 14.11 | 13.12 | 12.1* |
| 1994 | 10.2 | 12.3 | 11.4 | 11.5 | 9.6 | 9.7 | 7.8 | 6.9 | 5.10 | 3.11 | 3.12 | 1.1* |
| 1995 | 31.1 | 1.3 | 31.3 | 30.4 | 29.5 | 28.6 | 27.7 | 26.8 | 24.10 | 22.11 | 22.12 | 20.1* |
| 1996 | 19.2 | 19.3 | 18.4 | 17.5 | 16.6 | 16.7 | 14.8 | 13.9 | 12.10 | 11.11 | 11.12 | 9.1* |
| 1997 | 7.2 | 9.3 | 7.4 | 7.5 | 5.6 | 5.7 | 3.8 | 2.9 | 2.10 | 31.10 | 30.11 | 30.12 |
| 1998 | 28.1 | 27.2 | 28.3 | 26.4 | 26.5 | 23.7 | 22.8 | 21,9 | 20.10 | 19.11 | 19.12 | 17.1* |
| 1999 | 16.2 | 18.3 | 16.4 | 15.3 | 14.6 | 13.7 | 11.8 | 10.9 | 9.10 | 8.11 | 8.12 | 7.1* |
| 2000 | 5.2 | 6.3 | 5.3 | 4.5 | 2.6 | 2.7 | 31.7 | 29.8 | 28.9 | 27.10 | 26.11 | 26.12 |
| 2001 | 24.1 | 23.2 | 25.3 | 23.4 | 21.6 | 21.7 | 19.8 | 17.9 | 17.10 | 15.11 | 15.12 | 13.1* |
| 2002 | 12.2 | 14.3 | 12.4 | 12.5 | 6.6 | 10.7 | 8.8 | 7.9 | 6.10 | 4.11 | 4.12 | 2.1* |
| 2003 | 1.2 | 3.3 | 1.4 | 1.5 | 31.5 | 29.6 | 29.7 | 27.8 | 26.9 | 25.10 | 23.11 | 12.12 |
| 2004 | 22.1 | 20.2 | 19.4 | 19.5 | 18.6 | 17.7 | 16.8 | 14.9 | 14.10 | 12.11 | 12.12 | 10.1* |
| 2005 | 9.2 | 10.3 | 9.4 | 8.5 | 7.6 | 6.7 | 5.8 | 4.9 | 3.10 | 2.11 | 1.12 | 1.1* |
| 2006 | 29.1 | 28.2 | 29.3 | 28.4 | 27.5 | 26.6 | 25.7 | 22.9 | 22.10 | 21.11 | 20.12 | 19.1* |
| 2007 | 18.2 | 19.3 | 17.4 | 17.5 | 15.6 | 14.7 | 13.8 | 11.9 | 11.10 | 10.11 | 10.12 | 8.1* |
| 2008 | 7.2 | 8.3 | 6.4 | 5.5 | 4.6 | 3.7 | 1.8 | 31.8 | 29.9 | 29.10 | 28.11 | 27.12 |
| 2009 | 27.1 | 25.2 | 27.3 | 25.4 | 24.5 | 22.7 | 20.8 | 19.9 | 18.10 | 17.11 | 16.12 | 15.1* |
| 2010 | 14.2 | 16.3 | 14.4 | 14.5 | 12.6 | 12.7 | 10.8 | 8.9 | 8.10 | 6.11 | 6.12 | 4.1* |
| 2011 | 3.2 | 5.3 | 3.4 | 3.5 | 2.6 | 1.7 | 31.7 | 29.8 | 27.9 | 27.10 | 25.11 | 25.12 |
| 2012 | 23.1 | 22.2 | 22.3 | 21.4 | 19.6 | 19.7 | 17.8 | 16.9 | 15.10 | 14.11 | 13.12 | 12.1* |
| 2013 | 10.2 | 12.3 | 10.4 | 10.5 | 8.6 | 8.7 | 7.8 | 15.9 | 5.10 | 3.11 | 3.12 | 1.1* |
| 2014 | 1.2 | 1.3 | 31.3 | 29.4 | 29.5 | 27.6 | 27.7 | 25.8 | 24.9 | 22.11 | 12.12 | 20.1* |
| 2015 | 19.2 | 20.3 | 29.4 | 18.5 | 16.6 | 16.7 | 14.8 | 13.9 | 13.10 | 12.11 | 22.12 | 10.1* |
| 2016 | 9.2 | 9.3 | 7.4 | 7.5 | 5.6 | 4.7 | 1.8 | 1.9 | 1.10 | 31.10 | 29.11 | 29.12 |
| 2017 | 28.1 | 26.2 | 28.3 | 26.4 | 26.5 | 24.6 | 22.8 | 20.9 | 20.10 | 18.11 | 18.12 | 17.1* |
| 2018 | 16.2 | 17.3 | 16.4 | 15.5 | 14.6 | 13.7 | 11.8 | 10.9 | 9.10 | 8.11 | 7.12 | 6.1* |

* the date refers to the January of the following years

| | | | |
|---|---|---|---|
| 1st | Zhēngyuè (Start Month) | 7th | Qiǎoyuè (Skill Month) |
| 2nd | Xìngyuè (Apricot Month) | 8th | Guìyuè (Osmanthus Month) |
| 3rd | Táoyuè (Peach Month) | 9th | Júyuè (Chrysanthemum Month) |
| 4th | Huáiyuè (Locust Tree Month) | 10th | Yángyuè (Yang Month) |
| 5th | Púyuè (Sweet Sedge Month) | 11th | Dōngyuè (Winter Month |
| 6th | Héyuè (Lotus Month) | 12th | Làyuè (Preserved Month) |

# A menagerie of different characters

As with western astrology, one of the main ways in which the Chinese put their beliefs into practice is to ascribe different personality traits to each sign, map out the future of those born under them and see which signs are compatible in romantic matters and which should be avoided. With a population of over one billion, each sign applies to between 800 and 900 million Chinese and considerably more of the rest of us. What follows then can only be general, extremely general, although the author (a Rooster) recognized something of himself in that section, and when he took into account the influence of his Moon month, he was more than a little impressed!

# The Rat

Charming, appealing, clever, quick-witted and sociable are all adjectives that the Chinese ascribe to the Rat – a creature regarded as wise in Oriental mythology. Their habit of scurrying around in the dark gave rise to the widespread belief that they had occult powers. Rats, with their natural curiosity and inquisitive nature, seem to want to know as much as they can about absolutely everything.

Those born under the sign have the ability to talk the hind legs off a donkey and they can write with impressive fluency. But they have a practical nature and are adaptable, having the ability to turn their hand to most things. They are party animals, especially at New Year. They enjoy life in the fast lane and are inveterate gamblers, not just at the tables but in love and in business, too.

But all this feverish social activity has a down side, disguising as it does the Rats' insecurity. They have a deep-rooted fear of not being loved, which is why they play the field in the romance stakes. They are also afraid that one day they may run out of the money they need to finance their lifestyles, which is why they squirrel away money in savings accounts to make sure that should that rainy day come, they won't get too wet.

In matters of health, the Rats' reliance on themselves can produce stress and their liking for an active social life can temp them into an unhealthy diet that can lead to raised cholesterol levels and all that that entails.

When it comes to matters sexual and the affairs of the heart, Rats can be obsessive about sex and often form hot, hot, hot relationships with Dragons. But when the fires of passion die down, Rats often find themselves seeking solace in the arms of a Pig or an Ox, with whom they often form long-lasting relationships. Rats can find themselves attracted to Horses and Monkeys, but the speed of the former and the

capriciousness of the latter tend to ensure that the flames of passion are soon doused.

The Moon months affect Rats in the following way: Those born during the first Moon are sensitive and like nothing better than initiating new ideas, the more controversial the better. The next Moon makes those born during its rule introspective to the point that others see them as indifferent to everything. Rats who owe the third Moon their loyalty will do anything to be different, while those who enter the world during the succeeding Moon are the sort of people who, when they have an idea, will stick to it come thick or thin. To succeed in life they have to be more flexible. The fifth Moon blesses its followers with an artistic nature, which allows them to express their emotions more than most. Those born during the sixth Moon love the good things in life, and make no secret about it. They have boundless enthusiasm, something that makes them excellent salesmen. To be born under the seventh Moon usually makes one something of a prevaricator, but if they take a lead from the title of the Shakespeare play *All's Well That Ends Well* they will be fine. They may, though, look with envy on those who are blessed by the eighth Moon being in the night sky when they are born: for such people have brains, looks and good fortune. But brains must be used if they are to stay in good fettle, looks fade and good fortune can turn to bad. The ninth Moon makes those who owe it allegiance over-concerned with the minutiae of life. If they can be chivied into taking the wider view, their lives will be enriched beyond measure. Those born under the tenth Moon are great gamblers, often lucky ones. And therein lies their downfall. For flushed with early success they over-reach themselves and can end up in the gutter (although they will, in the words of Oscar Wilde, be looking at stars). The second-to-last Moon encourages an interested mind – the trouble is its interest knows no bounds and when coupled with a lack of concentration, often leads to a butterfly mind. The final Moon of the year whose demise heralds the dawn of the Year of the Ox lends a tendency to stubbornness that must be overcome if success in life, both personal and professional, is to be achieved.

## The Ox

A dependable beast of burden and in some cultures regarded as a symbol of fertility, the Ox arrives early in the year, bringing with it the good news that spring is just around the corner.

People born in the year of the Ox are sometimes seen as being as slow as the animal itself, but they are intelligent and, with their affinity for the outside world, they often

have a deep concern about the environment. They love their homes and need them to provide a stable base for themselves and their families.

But they have their faults – which of us don't? They can be stubborn and sullen: once their mind is made up, little if anything will change it. Just as the animal will plough furrow after furrow, oblivious to any outside distraction, so those born under this sign are naturally blinkered. And they can be possessive to the point of obsessiveness.

They make excellent team workers and are unlikely ever to stand accused of not pulling their weight. They are meticulous planners and possess the enviable ability of pondering over plans when the rest of us have long gone to bed, while at the same time energizing themselves for whatever the next day holds.

Oxen born during the first Moon are, due to the influence of the departing Rat, often less stubborn and more self-confident than others of the sign. The second Moon blesses Oxen with a creativity that can become so intense that they become unusually introspective, finding it difficulty to form relationships with others. Those born under the succeeding Moon tend to need constant reminding that things are not as bad as they might look, and that they should get out more and mix with others. When the fourth Moon reigns, her subjects tend to be deep-thinkers, so deep that thinking is all they do and they have to be nudged into making conclusions. This is not something that can be said about anyone born during the fifth Moon, for they are quick-witted, if a bit slapdash. The sixth Moon bestows a youthful quality on her subjects, too youthful for some, who have eventually to be reminded that there is nothing to be ashamed of in growing old gracefully. Her sister, the seventh Moon, lends those on whom she shines a cool, oh so cool exterior, which is deceptive, for beneath it lies an unusually active and very creative mind. Those born under the eighth Moon are also deceptive, for although they seem to be party animals, what they really crave is a night at home with the object of their affections. Generosity is the keyword that can be applied to those who come into the world when the ninth Moon is in the ascendant, and although this quality is often exploited by others, their generosity is eventually rewarded. When the ninth Moon gives way to the tenth, generosity bows to self-reliance and it is no surprise to learn that many successful self-employed people are born during this phase of the Moon. The succeeding Moon makes those in her realm hungry for power, but that doesn't stop them from being thoughtful and considerate friends. Alas this cannot be said for those born under the last Moon, for while they, too, love power, they tend to be loners and find it hard to take criticism.

When it comes to trying to make sure that their relationships with others are well balanced, the Ox can become obsessive. Roosters and Dragons are only too happy to put up with, indeed encourage this. But Tigers and Pigs are usually far too aggressive for the Ox.

Oxen have a sweet tooth and their tendency to overeat can cause problems. They are sensitive to extremes of temperature which they find cause them discomfort in the stomach and chest.

## The Tiger

Those born under the sign of the Tiger tend to be extremely competitive and very brave. They enjoy the charisma that they are aware they exude and although they tend to be loners in some aspects of their lives, they see themselves as natural leaders, for they think themselves naturally superior to us lesser mortals. They can be among the most philanthropic of people, but whereas some others do good by stealth, Tigers enjoy having their efforts noticed.

The 'smile on the face of the tiger' mentioned in the famous limerick, belies its fearsome bite and the sense of calm that the tiger projects gives no hint of the energy that is simmering under the surface, waiting to be released. Conquest is the name of their game, be it in their business lives or in their personal relationships.

Unlike those born under some other signs who find it hard to keep two balls in the air at the same time, the Tiger can juggle a seemingly endless number, managing several projects simultaneously with effortless ease. But this ease belies a curious contradiction. Others may see

the Tiger as a menace, but not as much of a menace as the Tiger sees itself! It craves safety and finds it in its home, which is almost certain to be lavishly, some may even say ostentatiously, furnished.

Tigers are at their best in the early spring when they leave their winter lair and seek out new territories to conquer. Those born under the first Moon can, thanks to the lingering influence of the Ox, be more reserved than other Big Cats, but will often act out of character and behave as flamboyantly as the others. Those born under the second Moon often stand accused of speaking their minds in too forthright a manner, for they overreact to people and events. The third Moon has a tendency to make her subjects generous, daring and loving – sadly often over-generous, over-daring and over-loving for their own good. Tigers who bow to the fourth Moon have infectious personalities but are often easily tempted to stray from the path of marital faithfulness. When the fifth Moon rules the night sky, those born at that time are gloriously gregarious at some times yet shy from company at others. This makes them struggle to find the right balance. Tigers born during the next Moon often have to be constantly reassured that the doldrums in which they constantly find themselves will not last forever. The seventh Moon encourages straight dealing and through it success in the community. The most artistic Moon Month for Tigers is the eighth, and those born at this time often follow their instincts and take up an artistic career. Aesthetic is a word often used to describe Tigers born during the ninth Moon. Others may see Tigers born now as superficial, but are usually forced to revise their opinions when they get better acquainted with the subject of their approbation. The tenth Moon encourages her neonates to stick to what they want to do, ignoring any criticism and facing any problems that present themselves. Those born during the eleventh Moon often find themselves exhausted both mentally and physically because they are always in pursuit of ideals, while those born during the twelfth Moon are often seen as so self-confident that it rankles with others. But as long as the self-confidence doesn't turn to arrogance, they soon win others over.

When Tigers give their hearts, it is often to fellow felines who share their intensity of feeling. Problems can arise though, because of the Tiger's surprising passivity in romance and tendency to be unfaithful. The one sign Tigers should avoid is the Pig – far too nervous to snuggle up to a big cat.

The Tiger's over-confidence can make them take on far too much, which can cause symptoms of stress that the sleek animal often ignores until it is too late and the damage has been done.

# The Rabbit

Curiously contradictory in character, gay and gregarious
at some times, party wallflowers at others, they seem to
have come into the world with an inborn fear of getting
involved and when any sort of confrontation looms, they
try to dig themselves into a burrow until it's gone. If you
know someone who observes silently on the sidelines
of any social gathering, and then is first on the phone
for a good gossip – that's a Rabbit. Like their animal
counterparts, they are the great breeders of the Zodiac
menagerie. It's family first and although they may roam
far from home, they can't wait to scurry back to the warren
– and usually one they have lived in for a long time, for if
there's one thing a Rabbit hates, it's upheaval.

They have a wily intelligence, which they wield with
great skill to get them out of sticky situations. They hoard
things like no other sign and ask a Rabbit to go shopping
with you and they will drop what they're doing and help
you spend, spend, spend, only too happy to join you in
melting the plastic.

Rabbits make great friends and excellent business
partners. Not the most sensual of animals, they relish
long-term relationships with partners who will grow and
mature alongside them. Rats and Oxen are the signs best
suited to cope with the Rabbit's ways, Snakes will exhaust
them emotionally and fellow Rabbits are far too elusive to
allow themselves to be snared.

First Moon Rabbits have an extra confidence and are
first to dive in at the deep end and get their plans, which
are usually straightforward, off the ground, whereas
those born under the next one tend to scurry hither and
thither before making up their minds about anything.
The third Moon blesses her subjects with a decisive mind
and when she hands over to her sister, the fourth, she

encourages others to feel protective towards her children who sometimes have to struggle before they come to accept this. Indecision is the curse of those born under the fifth Moon, while those with birthdays during the one that follows appear the very model of conformity on the outside, while being true lotus-eaters on the inside. If they can let their inner self come to the surface sometimes, their lives will be all the richer for it. Those who owe allegiance to the seventh Moon are blessed with creativity in all things artistic, have good business brains and make excellent politicians – if only they can stir themselves out of their elegant ennui! The eighth Moon smiles eternal optimism on those who owe their loyalty to her: if someone were to raise the *Titanic*, they'd be first in line to buy a ticket for its maiden voyage. Rabbits born when the ninth Moon reigns are obsessive hoarders – valuable or not, useful or absolutely redundant, you name it, they'll store it somewhere. Tenth Moon Rabbits are loners, the sort of people in whose vocabulary the words 'team' and 'spirit' have absolutely no connection whatsoever. Their cousins born under the penultimate Moon will stop at nothing apart from betrayal to get what they want and those on whom the last Moon smiles draw on the energy of the approaching Dragon which gives them the drive to succeed at whatever they decide to do.

# The Dragon

To the Ancient Chinese, the Dragon crossed the skies and marked time's passing. A helpful creature, blessed with vitality and occult powers, it marked auspicious events from the birth of an heir to the death of a benefactor. People born under this sign are blessed with the same vitality. Their intuitive ability to understand any situation puts them in a position to influence events. But the influence that they bring to bear may not be what is wanted, something that is more often than not due to the fact that many of them have their heads in the clouds.

Dragons have such self-confidence that they often delude themselves into believing that their middle name is 'Infallible'. They will start projects and relationships with boundless, youthful enthusiasm, only to abandon them halfway through when their impetuosity drives them off in another direction. Their superficial show of bravado often disguises an insecurity, which the Dragon will go to great lengths to cover with a wide smile or an expensive new outfit.

They have so much energy that trying to channel it can become their main preoccupation in life. This explains the frustration they feel when things don't go their way,

a frustration that can cause outbursts of volcanic temper, when they seem to spit fire with every word.

Dragons need love and affection, things that the Rooster is only too happy to offer. The Snake, too. Surprisingly, the Tiger and the Dragon being opposites in many respects, can be an excellent match. The Horse tends to be too devious, and Dragons who find themselves attracted to a Dog will soon find that they are barking up the wrong tree.

Like all other signs, the Dragon's temperament is influenced by the lunar month in which he or she is born. The lingering influence of the Rabbit makes Dragons born during the first Moon more introspective than other Dragons. This is something that engenders suspicion about the typically creative ideas that flood from this and all Dragons. Second Moon Dragons breeze through life with a smile on their face that belies the inner turmoil churning up their stomachs. The third Moon invigorates her subjects with the knowledge that life is for living and the stamina to do just that, while those born during the fourth Moon make no concessions to anyone or anything. They are what they are – like them or lump them. Dragons who first breathe fire during the fifth Moon are blessed with great powers of concentration that allow them to get to the end of the road, no matter how bumpy the ride. Those born when the next Moon illumines the night sky are fireballs of creative energy that brands itself on all who cross their path. People who know Dragons born under the seventh Moon often have reason to be grateful to them for the confidence and trust they inspire. The eighth Moon makes her subjects extremely logical and engenders in them the need to set their sights on a definite goal before they set out on any project. This is not something that many will say about ninth-Moon Dragons with their head in the clouds and chiffon-soft ideas. But what others don't realize is that some of the greatest inventions, most brilliant books and beautiful paintings have been the children of dreamers. The eponymous creature lies very deep within Dragons born during the tenth Moon, but don't be deceived by the placid exterior: it's there, ready to breathe fire whenever necessary. The second-to-last Moon blesses (or curses) her children with a will to win that overrides everything else in life. Dragons who look to the last Moon are cool and sophisticated, but there's a hot, passionate slumbering person beneath just waiting to be awakened.

## The Snake

Hypnotic and charming. Wise but naïve. Prudent, profligate and possessive, with more than a touch of

prudery thrown in. The word 'contradiction' could have been invented for Snakes. They lie in wait, biding their time until it is time to act, no matter how long it takes. Those who see this as inactivity do so at their peril, for the Snake is planning the next move – right down to the last detail. Snakes absorb information, gathering intelligence with the same appetite with which a glutton attacks his food, then sieve it and put it in the right compartment of their super-intelligent minds. Facts may be their diet, but they have the ability to cook up original ideas, especially artistic ones. Sometimes, in putting their brains into overdrive, their judgements might be unbalanced and the answers they come up with to solve problems can be off-target. Not that the Snake will see this.

Their love of companionship encourages them to stay as close to home as they can. But their love of the creative arts can overcome this and see them venturing forth. They are the late risers of the Chinese Zodiac, often staying in bed when the rest of us are up and about. But the Snake is conserving its energy and planning the day ahead.

Craving love and affection, in matters of romance, Snakes are well matched with the Dragon or the considerate Dog. The Rat will play with a Snake's emotion and while the Tiger has its attractions, it is too prone to betrayal for the Snake ever to be truly comfortable.

Snakes hatched during the first Moon should heed the warning that while acquiring knowledge is a good thing, too much of it, like too little, can be a dangerous thing. Those born when the second Moon shines need to be counselled not to bottle things up: a problem shared is a problem halved. When the third Moon is in the sky, her subjects often have the confidence to follow a freelance career, with the caveat that over-confidence has been the downfall of many. Fourth Moon snakes tend to think of themselves too much and need to be encouraged to take a more relaxed view of life. Snakes loyal to the fifth Moon have an instinctive and enviable eye for the good things in life, material and spiritual. Sixth-Moon Snakes have a cautious mind, which can be used to help others who have a tendency to live in the clouds come down to earth. When the seventh Moon shines it invigorates her subjects, making them especially active and allowing them to scale the highest peaks. Those born under the eighth Moon often find themselves tripping over their aggressive self-confidence. This is tempered during the next one, whose people are outgoing and gregarious with the happy knack of making friends wherever they go. The tenth Moon brings with it an especially strong tendency to repress things. Snakes born now should learn to let go more often. The penultimate Moon bestows a talent for organizing all manner of things in general, social events in particular, and for communicating, and the last one, being influenced by the imminent arrival of the Horse, makes Snakes born now more direct and adventurous than their sibling serpents.

# The Horse

Those born under the Horse are all-rounders, as sociable, sporting, hard-working and well-travelled as the animal itself. The downside? They can develop strong prejudices, become selfish and intolerant.

Their endless vitality and energy can drive them on to do almost anything they set their mind to, leaving the rest of us at the starting post, watching with just a hint of envy as luck smiles again and again on the thoroughbred of the Chinese Zodiac. To the Horse, life is a game, which is played constantly on the attack: the word 'defence' is not in his vocabulary but the word 'winner' is, and that is what he strives to be.

But the Horse is just as willing to pick up the cudgel and use his strengths to help friends fight their battles. For despite their independent streak, they are good team-players as long as they can keep their instinctive desire to be captain at bay. They take the overall view, leaving the details to others. That can lead to the Horse's downfall: charging ahead, head held high and attention firmly focused on the goalposts, he often fails to clear the details that present themselves as hurdles in his path. And when things don't go according to plan, the Horse will be just as hard on others as he will be on himself.

Often as strong physically as they are mentally, Horses are practical and handy to have around the house. When they settle down it is often with the extrovert Tiger or the outgoing Dragon. Rarely will a Horse be happy with

a Ram (too methodical) or the Monkey (unsettlingly restless).

Horses born during the first Moon find success early in life, and so it continues. Those born under the next Moon are too independent and have to be reined in to work with people. Third Moon horses need all the friends they have, and more. When the fourth Moon rises, it shines on the intellect and artistic abilities. Fifth Moon horses have a tendency to show off the fruits of their labours, something that irks others and has to be discouraged. Sixth Moon ones have a deep-rooted need for security and in their search for it often hop from person to person regardless of the hurt this causes. Horses born during the seventh Moon are especially lucky and self-reliant. When the eighth Moon shines, she brings a generous spirit but a tendency to over-indulge. 'Look before you leap,' are words to which Horses born under the ninth Moon should pay particular attention, for the barriers between them and the success they crave are often ones of their own making. Tenth Moon Horses often find it hard to communicate with others and should learn to loosen the reins. Their stablemates born during the eleventh Moon have a stronger capacity for analytical thinking than other Horses. It's something that they find useful when times are hard. The up-coming Ram tempers the Horses' headstrong ways. Horses born under the twelfth Moon are the stayers in the race to success – reserving some power for a final gallop to victory after enjoying an easy canter behind the leaders.

## The Ram

Rams are orderly creatures who like everything to be in its proper place. Conservative with a small 'c' (and often with a large one) and with a firm belief that everything that has to be done can be done if only the correct method can be found. And oh, the fear of failure if they can't find it. Rams are the realists of the Chinese Zodiac. When they set themselves a target it will be a realistic one: no pie in the sky promises from Rams, nothing over ambitious.

Well-meaning if a little dull, Rams like things to run smoothly, not just for themselves, but for their friends and colleagues for whom they will move heaven and earth to ensure a trouble-free path through life, even if this does seem a little interfering at times. A businessman in search of a perfect secretary could do no better than look to the sheep pen for help.

Being canny creatures, Rams are masters of the waiting game, biding their time and only acting when they judge the time to be right. The word 'inspiring' is not one that

could be applied to most Rams: but when it comes to researching the best way to plan for the future, Rams are non-pareil. If you are working to a tight deadline, don't ask a Ram for help. If something has to be delayed before it is ready to go, then so be it.

They are home-loving creatures who like nothing more than throwing parties, not just because they enjoy acting the host, but also because they like showing off the homes they have made for themselves. They make firm friends, but friendships are slow to turn to intimacy when love rears its head. They are happy with other Rams and with Horses, one of the few signs able to get through the Ram's reserve. Oxen are far too bovine for Rams, who are often attracted to Rats – but not for long.

Rams born during the first Moon, inherit some of the power of the preceding Horse, something they can use to their advantage to help them win looming battles, especially career ones. Those born when the second Moon reigns have to work hard to come to terms with the fact that upheavals can derail even the best-laid plans. Third Moon Rams are especially cerebral, often to the point that it makes them blind to more mundane matters. Rams who owe loyalty to the fourth Moon are the most sensual and social of sheep, assets they use to get what they want and those on whom the fifth Moon shines are often at their most relaxed at parties where they can mix with others and enjoy wide-ranging conversations. That can't be said for Rams born during the sixth phase: often too deep in thought, they have to be continually prodded into being more outgoing. Seventh Moon Rams enjoy the good things in life, not just for themselves, but for their friends, too. Rams who bleat for the first time during the eighth Moon are great worriers, often deeply suspicious of everyone else's motives. 'Control' and 'freak' are words that combine to describe Rams born during the ninth Moon. The serious front they present to the world conceals an even more serious interior. Tenth Moon Rams often fail to see the wood for the confusing trees in their sight. They have to be assured not only that there is a path through, but that they will find it. Rams born during the penultimate Moon are hugely house-proud, oblivious to the fact that taken to the extreme it puts people off. And with Monkey waiting in the wings, Rams born during the last Moon are the most frivolous in the flock.

## The Monkey

Watching a monkey in the wild, one can only wonder at their agility, their audacity and their constant activity. All of which has to take its toll in the end, which is when they

slump, exhausted and unmoving. It's the same with their Zodiac counterparts. Always on the go, inventive and great fun to be with, they are often plunged into periods when they feel insecure and depressed. But not for long. That irrepressible sense of fun soon re-emerges and they're off again, cajoling the rest of us to loosen up and have fun. They can be outrageously flirtatious and manipulative, but they really do love their fellows and their intentions are usually good.

Don't be fooled by the madcap behaviour. Monkeys know exactly what they're doing: they know what they want and usually get it. And if they have to play games with people to do so, such is their nature that when they are caught out, they are usually forgiven. They are on the go for days on end, and then they'll slump, gather their energy and start again, fidgeting and fussing and generally interfering with other people's lives – usually for the common good, though.

The Ox will put up with the Monkey's hyperactivity, and the Rat makes a good partner, too, being able to calm the Monkey and encourage it to enjoy a little domesticity. Horses and Monkeys tap into the same energy source, but they will never settle down together – far too exhausting a pairing.

First Moon Monkeys are real charmers, an asset they often use to organize others. Second Moon ones enjoy hoarding things so much that it can become an obsession. Monkeys born during the third Moon have butterfly minds and have to be coaxed into concentration if they are to achieve their true potential. Those who first see the light of day when the fourth Moon shines have a tendency to cockiness and need to be told that they can achieve their ambitions just as easily if they learn a little humility. Curiously, fifth Moon Monkeys need to be coaxed into talking about their achievements and while vanity is one thing, there's nothing wrong with a little pride. Monkeys born during the sixth Moon have an abundance of confidence matched with talents that assure them of success in whatever direction they choose to travel. Their cousins who are born during the next Moon are excellent communicators, who often find satisfaction in politics and show business. When the eighth Moon is in the sky, her Monkeys often find themselves side-tracked by trivial details. If those born during the ninth one can be encouraged periodically to shrug off the cloak of experience and see things through fresh eyes, their lives will be all the better for it. Tenth Moon Monkeys tend to have minds that never settle and have to be forced to concentrate on things and get themselves organized if they are to fulfil their true potential. Monkeys born during the second-to-last Moon are cool, calm and collected, especially in managing businesses and arranging things for others, while those who owe allegiance to the final Moon have in spades the Monkey's tendency to move from place to place, person to person, job to job. They have to be urged to settle down or they will exhaust themselves and their partners.

## The Rooster

A natural leader, the Rooster is alert to new opportunities and is usually the first to see a problem looming on the horizon. Others often see the Rooster as over-confident, cocksure, forever crowing about their own achievements, abrasive and over-competitive – and they are right. But the Rooster couldn't give a hoot. Sights set, the Rooster will get there – how is a minor consideration. And here is a seeming contradiction, for although in business they are hard taskmasters, they are often selfless employers who seem to have the best interest of their employees at heart. Don't be fooled! It's odds on that the Rooster started the business and is acting out of pure self-interest.

Watch a rooster in the coop. See how he confidently struts among the chickens, enjoying their admiration. The Rooster is just the same. With their extravagant appearance and matching behaviour, they shine at parties, especially if they have something new that evidences their success.

The good-natured Pig is a good match for the Rooster, and although, when attracted to another Rooster, the two will fight for dominance, harmony will soon replace aggression and the two will make a devoted couple. Roosters and Dogs don't make a good match – too distant – and although the Rabbit may seem a good partner, it won't last: the Rooster's traits will soon start to annoy

and he will be surprised at the aggression with which the Rabbit reacts to this.

But, as usual, the Mansions of the Moon influence things. Roosters born during the first Moon tend to be less aggressive, more willing to listen, than others of the brood. Second Moon Roosters are often tempted to sit at home, planning and organizing things on their own. They should resist this and get out more. Those born during the third Moon are especially good at recognizing the potential of new projects and then getting them up and running. When the fourth Moon is in the sky, her Roosters are prone to be over-ponderous about scholarly matters and need to be nudged out of this. The fifth Moon ushers in a time of extremes. Roosters born during her ascendancy should use these to guide them towards their goals. Roosters loyal to the sixth Moon should enjoy basking in the warm sunshine and let it stimulate their success. When the seventh Moon rules the night sky she encourages her Roosters to see their imperfections and to use them to their advantage, something that makes these birds much less self-centred than other hatchlings. This Moon exerts her influence on her successor, something that makes eighth Moon Roosters good listeners and to know that there is such a word as modesty in the dictionary. Ninth Moon Roosters may appear to be unflappable, but they are often all aflutter beneath the feathers. Roosters who first crow during the tenth Moon are born with a great desire to collect things – anything – and try to fight it off. They shouldn't. They should surrender to their instincts and relish this trait. During the eleventh Moon, the Yin and the Yang are perfectly balanced, enabling Roosters born now to achieve their heart's desire through careful planning. And when the twelfth Moon glows, she is aware that she has to hand over to the Dog, something that strengthens the Rooster's natural friendliness.

# The Dog

Man's best friend – loyal, protective and fearless – lends all its characteristics to those born during its years of ascendancy in the Chinese Zodiac. They will get involved in things, often without thinking of the consequences they may have to face. What they want is results and they want them NOW! Not for them are lengthy periods of negotiation or discussion that loom endlessly ahead.

They are honest and straightforward, often with a seemingly placid nature that belies an underlying restlessness. They are steadfast in their friendships and make few enemies – but when they do, watch out! And being quick to show the affection they feel for others,

they make it easy for them to feel quite unembarrassed when demonstrating the feelings they return. They are optimistic, sometimes over-optimistic, which can result in disappointments. They simply don't understand it when a friendship goes awry, which is why they should on occasions sit back on their hindquarters and take stock of the world round them, their friends and possessions.

Dogs and Tigers, perhaps surprisingly for seeming opposites, often enjoy passionate affairs and sizzling long-term relationships, but Pigs are probably the best-matched creatures for the Dog. Rats are usually too nervous for the sociable canine and a match with an Ox is almost guaranteed to end in a battle of wills from which winner takes all.

Dogs born during the first Moon are often tempted to live for the day and have to be reminded that they

should look to the future. Those loyal to the second
Moon often find that the loyalty they feel for others
evaporates due to circumstances beyond their control.
Dogs who give voice to their bark for the first time when
the third Moon shines tend to be particularly persistent
creatures who are often found in the communications
industry. The fourth Moon encourages her denizens
to make others feel good: in doing so, they always feel
good themselves. Dogs born during the fifth Moon often
appear conceited and over-confident. That's nothing
to be ashamed of, for these dogs are every bit as good
as they think themselves to be. The sixth Moon blesses
her subjects with brains and the ability to get things
done that have proved impossible for others. Seventh
Moon subjects sometimes find themselves unable to
move forward for reasons they can't put their finger on.
Dogs born during the next Moon set themselves high
standards, and expect the same of others too. If these
are not met, these Dogs can bark too fiercely for their
own good. Ninth Moon dogs often feel instinctively that
others are acting against them, but such is their view of
life that they find this hard to believe. They should be
well-advised to change their perception of things and
take the appropriate action. This suspicion lingers on
during the reign of the tenth Moon and Dogs born now
are more prone to be the target of wagging tongues than
others in the kennel. Dogs during the second-to-last
Moon sometimes tend to be a little suspicious when
someone offers the paw of friendship. They needn't
be. By the time the twelfth Moon takes to the sky, the
up-coming Pig is starting to exert its influence, telling
Dogs that working consistently towards a goal is often
better than going for it in fits and starts.

# The Pig

The last sign in the twelve-year cycle, Pigs are born at a time when new horizons beckon. They are creative and intelligent and only too happy to take the world as they find it, something that explains the fact that the Pig is a contented animal. They are only too happy to use their intelligence for the benefit of others, for they are as generous as the day is long.

They often enjoy a lively social life, but at the end of the day, having joined in with gusto, they are only too happy to return to the sty. And therein lies a porcine problem. They like their homes so much that they can become over-anxious about finding the right partner to settle in it with. And when that particular person doesn't look like showing up, the Pig can become very, very depressed. The family is central to the Pig, and while they are happy for their offspring to leave home and make their own way in life, when it comes to coming home for Sunday lunch whenever possible, there's a three-line whip in operation.

Pigs and Rabbits make a good match, the latter's innate liveliness infecting the former to the Pig's advantage. And Dragons, provided they can be persuaded to calm down and enjoy a quieter life than they are used to, will make perfect partners for Pigs. Snakes and Pigs communicate on different wavelengths and a Horse will unseat a Pig at the first opportunity.

First Moon Pigs often enjoy success through hard work, while those born during the second Moon get it by the luck that shines upon them from the day they are born. The downside for them is that they tend to take this for granted, which leads them to become irritatingly over-confident. Ideas tumble from third Moon Pigs like snowflakes in a blizzard. These must be carefully sifted as not even the most diligent Pig has the ability to see them all through to successful fruition. Problems often appear during the middle years of Pigs born when the fourth Moon bathes the world in her glow, but these usually resolve themselves. Fifth Moon Pigs can be a little untrusting and might need to be advised that the world is a much nicer place than they think it is. Once Pigs loyal to the sixth Moon make up their minds, nothing will change them. That's why they should weigh up every option very carefully before pronouncing on anything, no matter how trivial. Their seventh Moon cousins have the knack of achieving great things, but only after they have brought a little chaos into everyone's lives. The eighth Moon can make her subjects more tense than other Pigs, so much so that they have to be forced to relax. The ninth Moon, too, can cause trouble, letting her Pigs get so bogged down in trivia that they let the important things slide. And then they worry about this so much that they tend to do nothing about anything. They, too, need to relax. Tenth Moon Pigs can be too willing to shoulder other people's problems, but this often has beneficial results for everyone. Those born during the penultimate Moon really believe that there is nothing that they cannot do. They are often right, but become quite exhausted in the attempt. And if there's one lesson that Pigs born during the twelfth Moon should take to heart, it's that they should share their myriad ideas with others. That way they are much less likely to make blunders and will bring home the bacon.

# The I Ching

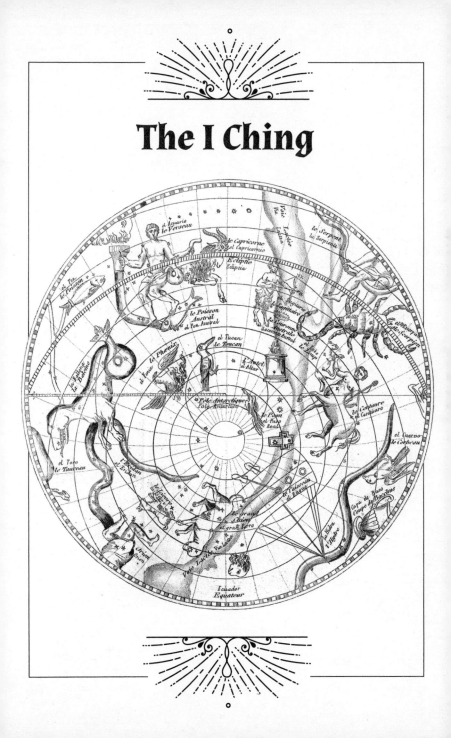

One legend has it that around 5000BC Fu Hsi, the first Chinese emperor, was meditating by a river when suddenly an animal that looked like some sort of dragon rose from the water. Fu Hsi, curious rather than scared, noticed that there were lines on its scales. Intrigued, he pondered on these lines and after a while felt that they helped him by making him a wiser man. A man of spirited generosity, he felt that if the animal had helped him it could help others and set about drawing a series of diagrams, a series of broken and unbroken lines, using the lines on the scales as his guide.

Another tale credits the same man, and dates the incident to around the same time and the same place, but has it that the animal in question was a tortoise – tortoise shells being a common means of divination.

The lines that Fu Hsi noted were the eight trigrams – a stack of three lines, each of which have specific attributes to the Earth, Mankind and Heaven. As with all things Chinese, the Yin and the Yang exerted their profound influence – the unbroken lines representing Yang, that controls Heaven, the day's activities, the Sun's heat, action and hardness. The broken lines are Yin, the feminine aspect that controls the Earth, the night's mystery, the cool Moon, softness and stillness.

Whichever of these (and other legends) is true is irrelevant: what matters is that the lines became the basis of I (pronounced 'ee') Ching, one of the most popular forms of divination in the East, and one that is increasing in popularity in the western world.

Thousands of years later, around 1150BC, the tyrant emperor Chou Sin imprisoned 'King' Wen, for what crime we know not. But during his seven-year imprisonment Wen refined the trigrams and devised the six-line hexagrams or kua and wrote a commentary for each.

While Wen was in prison, his eldest son Yu gathered together an army and overthrew Chou Sin. Yu became emperor in his place and bestowed on his father the title 'King', by which sobriquet he has been known ever since, even though he never ruled China.

When Yu died, he was succeeded by his brother Tan, the Duke of Chou, who had been thoroughly instructed in the I Ching by their father. It was he who interpreted the meanings of each of the individual lines and it was at this point, around 1100BC that the I Ching was considered complete.

One of the earliest methods of using the I Ching was to heat a tortoise until its shell cracked and to interpret the cracks that appeared! Fortunately we have moved on since then, and today there is more than one method.

Traditionalists use yarrow sticks to cast the I Ching. This is hugely complicated and involves fifty stalks of yarrow, one of which is set aside, and manipulating the remaining forty-nine stalks in four stages of operation. These four operations are repeated three times to form a line, and as there are six lines, 72 steps are required for the whole process. A time-consuming method.

Given the complexity of the yarrow method, it was inevitable that a simpler method of casting a hexagram would develop, and today the most common way of casting a hexagram, is to use coins – 'the Heavenly Pennies'. Some people strike a balance between the ultra-traditionalism of the yarrow and the upstart coins, by using specially made I Ching stones, which are marked with either a Yin or a Yang symbol. Traditionalists need not worry. The means may vary, but the interpretation remains the same, harking back across the millennia to Ancient China.

The method is simple. Take three coins and throw them down together, each throw forming a hexagram line. Chinese coins were inscribed on one side only and had a hole in the middle so that they could be threaded together. The inscribed side was Yin, the plain side was Yang. Modern coins are inscribed on both sides. For the purpose of the I Ching, the 'tails' side is allied to the inscribed side and is therefore Yin: the 'heads' side is assumed to be blank and therefore 'Yang'.

# The Eight Trigrams

Formalized by Fu Hsi, the eight trigrams are the basis of the sixty-four hexagrams, which are all the possible double combinations of the trigrams.

 Ch'ien represents Heaven, the Sun and the creation of all things. Triple Yang is represented by its three unbroken lines and promises vitality, an upsurge in fortune and new opportunities on the horizon. It promises harmonious times.

 K'un is the Earth and everything that is feminine. With three broken lines, Yan times three, it is the opposite of Ch'ien, but in a positive way. It speaks of softness, of emerging from the dark, of a pliant, passive nature that indicates devotion and harmony.

Chen is Thunder, bursting with new ideas. It is regeneration and new life. But it can be disturbing. Its two broken and one solid line point to holding back and changes in the offing. But it can also indicate a tendency to making hasty decisions, of acting before thinking.

 Sun, with its two solid lines and one broken one, is the Wind. All about marriage, procreation and birth, its soothing influence makes the ideal atmosphere for all things creative from ideas for new ventures to planting seeds for the next harvest.

 K'an, the sign of rushing, flowing Water, but running water can become a dangerous torrent. So beware of what lies beneath the surface: the threatening undercurrents at home and at work, which might well bring a flood of insecurity and a maelstrom of melancholy.

 Li, Fire, has vibrant qualities of awareness and understanding, and of leadership, too. It is the sign of the victorious warrior, of the all-conquering lover. But victory can go to the head, and remember that pride comes before the fall!

 Ken, Mountain, promises security and achievements built on solid foundations. Associated with mountains, it brings with it clear-sightedness and articulation, but it has hints of the hoarder and the hermit, as well as of relationships about to come to an end. It can also point to miserliness and a stubborn nature.

 Tui, Lake, is associated with friendly waters that fertilize the ground. Tui represents deep, unfulfilled desires that may be about to surface and bring a change in the way things are perceived. But it can warn against overindulgence and a tendency to obsessiveness.

# Creating the hexagrams

These then are the basis of the sixty-four hexagrams, which are, nowadays usually cast using coins. Before this is done, the question to be answered should be carefully framed in the mind. Most practitioners create a relaxing atmosphere, perhaps mellow lighting and perhaps breathing in fragrant incense. The more particular the question, the more detailed the answer that I Ching will yield.

Only when the question has been thoroughly pondered upon, should the coins be cast to create a hexagram, which is built from the bottom up. Very often, the answer to one question leads to another, but again, this should be thoroughly focused on before the second (and subsequent) hexagrams are created.

Take three coins of the same denomination. If they have no obvious 'heads' or 'tails' decide which side is to be so ascribed. The lines they create when cast are as follows:

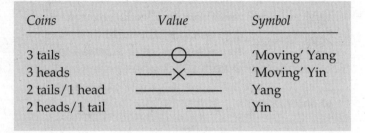

| Coins | Value | Symbol |
| --- | --- | --- |
| 3 tails | ———○——— | 'Moving' Yang |
| 3 heads | ———✕——— | 'Moving' Yin |
| 2 tails/1 head | ——————— | Yang |
| 2 heads/1 tail | ——— ——— | Yin |

The first throw gives the first line, the second the second one and so on, until a six-line hexagram has been created. As the hexagram is being built, mark each line on a piece of paper. Initially, the moving lines are read as if they were ordinary Yin and Yang ones. But once the hexagram has been built, moving lines are reversed in meaning: a 'Moving' Yin line becomes an unbroken Yang line, and a 'Moving' Yang line becomes a broken Yin one.

Historically, changing lines have the following significance. A changing first line points to a problem or a change that cannot find a solid foundation. A changing second line indicates instability. The third line suggests change due to shifts in time that cannot have been foreseen. The fourth line can point to change brought about by another's involvement, while the fifth points to beneficial changes brought about by an advancement of some kind. And the sixth says that the situation regarding the question is unbalanced.

The *I Ching* or *The Book of Changes*, the Chinese manuscript in which the meanings of the sixty-four hexagrams are explained, is a work of intense beauty. Each hexagram is described and explained line by line in the words of the philosopher. The most worthy translation is probably that of Richard Wilhelm and Cary F. Baynes, which was published by the Princeton University Press in 1967. Space precludes us, in this book, from going into the hexagrams in the exquisite detail that was the luxury of Wilhelm and Baynes. Rather we shall, perforce, restrict ourselves to a few key words about each of the sixty-four, and assure those who are drawn to the I Ching that it is well worth further study.

## 1. Chi'en 1 – The Creative
Success is assured through the questioner's strength, power and persistence. Plans can be continued with confidence, as long as there is no overreaching or overstretching of resources.

## 2. K'un 1 – The Receptive
The future can be viewed with confidence, as things will happen, but in their own time. And as success may lie in other people's hands, the questioner is advised to be still, responsive and receptive to advice.

## 3. Chun – Initial Difficulty
Opportunities that present themselves should be viewed with care as they might spell danger. If help is needed, don't be afraid to ask for it. And as it's early days, take care, there's no need to act hastily.

## 4. Meng – Innocence
There may be a lack of experience or even wisdom, so listen to the advice of other, more worldly people and learn from it. Remain enthusiastic and don't give up whatever you do.

Ch'ien 1    Ch'ien 2    Chen    Chi Chi

Chia Jen    Chieh 2    Chien 1    Chien 2

Chin    Ching    Chun    Chung Fu

Feng    Fu    Heng    Chieh 1

Hsien    Hsiao Ch'u    Hsiao Kuo    Hsu

## 5. Hsu – Waiting

Patience is a virtue. After all, if you plant seeds in a cornfield, you don't expect to harvest them right away. Help will be at hand when the time is right, so don't force the pace and worry. Wait and be ready.

## 6. Sung – Connection

Compromise is the keyword at the moment. Impulsive action, arguments and aggressive behaviour are to be avoided. If criticism is offered accept it. Listen to advice and things will improve.

## 7. Shih – The Arrow

Ask for respect and it will be received. If promotion is desired it will come, but after a struggle and probably after receiving some good advice from a wiser, and generally more mature person.

## 8. Pi – Union

This is the time to build up strong bonds by sharing experiences with others. Help them and at the same time you will be helping yourself. Pi is also an indication of harmonious partnerships.

## 9. Hsiao Ch'u – Taming Force

Now is the time to use your strength and power to clear small blockages from your path so that you are ready for the future. And although times may be hard, be thankful for small mercies. Restraint may be called for.

## 10. Lui – Treading Carefully

Stick to the path you have chosen and press forward without hesitating.

## 11. T'ai – Tranquillity

Good fortune and harmony are all around, so enjoy them and share them with others. This is a good time for planning for the future and for steady progress, but beware of the temptation to act rashly.

## 12. P'I 1 – Stagnation

This is not the time to force the pace, even if you are sure that there are rewards to be had. Modesty is called for if the change in the air is to be turned to your advantage.

## 13. T'ung Jen – Companionship

There are rewards to be had from working with others as long as everyone sticks to the tasks that have been allotted to them. This is a time for sharing. It is also a time when travel is indicated.

## 14. Ta Yu – Great Possession

Work hard, lay down for the future and success is yours for the taking.

## 15. Ch'ien 2 – Humility

Be modest and others will give you the help you need. Harmony is everything and it is vital to remain tolerant of others no matter how bad their behaviour may appear to be.

## 16. Yu – Happiness

Sell yourself, without necessarily believing what you say. This is a good time to plan for the future, but remember that money isn't everything: spiritual health is just as important as a bulging wallet.

## 17. Sui – Following

Now is the time to take a back seat and let others take charge. Be as flexible as you can and avoid any conflict.

Take a relaxed view of things but without letting your goals slip from view.

## 18. Ku – Disruption

Honesty is the best policy, so think hard and when you move forward do so with care. If you have made mistakes in the past, now is the time to rectify them.

## 19. Lin – Approach

Let caution be your watchword, moving forward with care and considering the feelings of others more than you may have done. Rash decisions are especially costly at the moment and may make today's good fortune temporary.

## 20. Kuan – Observing

A good time to plan for the future and for looking beneath the surface at things. Joint ventures could pay unexpected dividends, especially if you watch, listen and learn.

## 21. Shih Ho – Biting Through

Be positive about the success that has been achieved. And don't let the negativity of others affect you. There may be a legal matter of some kind to sort out, but you can win – in other areas, too.

## 22. P'I 2 – Adornment

Keep a rein on spending, especially if you are trying to create an impression. There are probably things that need to be sorted out, but do so in small stages, for the time is not right for sweeping changes.

## 23. Po – Stripping Away

This is not the time for action for the odds are not in your favour. There are disruptions ahead and change in the air. So wait and do what is needed to cope with them.

## 24. Fu – Returning

Caution, particularly regarding anything new, is the watchword at the moment. It is a time for patience and for timing the path ahead. It also indicates that old energies will be refreshed and new ones appear.

## 25. Wu Wang – Correctness

Remember that everything has its limits – don't be tempted to go beyond them. Selflessness and simplicity are keywords at the moment. Remember that problems are usually of a temporary nature, so be ready for the time when they vanish.

## 26. Ta Ch'u – Taming Force

Work is hard and progress slow, but luck is on your side and success is on the way, especially if you learn from mistakes made in the past.

## 27. I 1 – Nourishment

Take care, not only about what you eat and drink, but about what you say, too. This is a time to build up strength, to bide your time and to keep ambitions very much in check.

## 28. Ta Kuo – Excess

This is a time for extraordinary action. The inner voice should be listened to. And success is there, waiting for you to grasp it.

## 29. K'an – The Deep

Take care and be on the lookout for pitfalls. Conflict is in the air: proceed with caution, but make sure that you do proceed. Have faith in yourself and all will be well.

| | | | |
|---|---|---|---|
| Huan | I 1 | I 2 | K'an |
| K'uei | K'un 1 | K'un 2 | Ken |
| Ko | Ku | Ku i | Kuan |
| Kuei Mei | Kou | Li | Lin |
| Luí | Lu 2 | Meng | Ming I |

## 30. Li – Fire

Success can often be had by recognizing one's limitations. Now is the time to put the intellect to use and to be calm but firm.

## 31. Hsein – Sensitivity

Be receptive to other people's ideas and try to keep feelings of envy at arm's length. Help others at every opportunity, but do so for genuine reasons, and don't try to rule the roost at the expense of someone else.

## 32. Heng – Persistence

Set your course and stay with it. Stick to traditional methods and avoid any rash behaviour. If others offer advice, listen to it.

## 33. Tun – Withdrawal

There may be trouble ahead, but if you judge the right time to withdraw from the situation and are practical, you will weather the storm.

## 34. Ta Chuang – The Power of Greatness

If you say something, be sure that you stick to what you promise. This is a time of good fortune. If you act wisely you will benefit from it.

## 35. Chin – Advancement

This is a time when honesty is the best policy and also time to think of others. Do so and there is promotion or/ and social advancement in the offing.

## 36. Ming I – Darkening of the Light

Try not to get bogged down by making too many plans. Keep to the few that you have and try not to get too down in the mouth if things go badly: they will soon get better.

## 37. Chia Jen – Family

Family matters are to the fore and it will probably be necessary to exercise authority. But try to do so fairly and with tolerance. Men may find that the wisest course of action is to let their partners take the driving seat for the time being.

## 38. K'uei – Opposition

Try to stay in tune with the Yin and the Yang by ironing out anything disruptive or inharmonious in your life. It is a good time for starting small projects, and remember that mighty oak trees grow from tiny acorns.

## 39. Chien 1 – Halting

There are hard times ahead, with problems on the horizon. The only way to solve them is to face them: do so without making a song and dance, just think about them.

## 40. Chieh 1 – Removing Obstacles

A time for action, but not in haste. Solve the problem facing you, put it behind you and get on with things, resisting the temptation to dwell on the past.

## 41. Sun 1 – Decrease

Cut back on spending but share what you have with others even if it means making sacrifices in one area of your life. If you do this willingly the gain will be yours in the end.

## 42. I 2 – Increase

Luck is on your side and you can make plans with confidence that they will be successful. You may make mistakes, but worry not. They will turn out to be to your benefit.

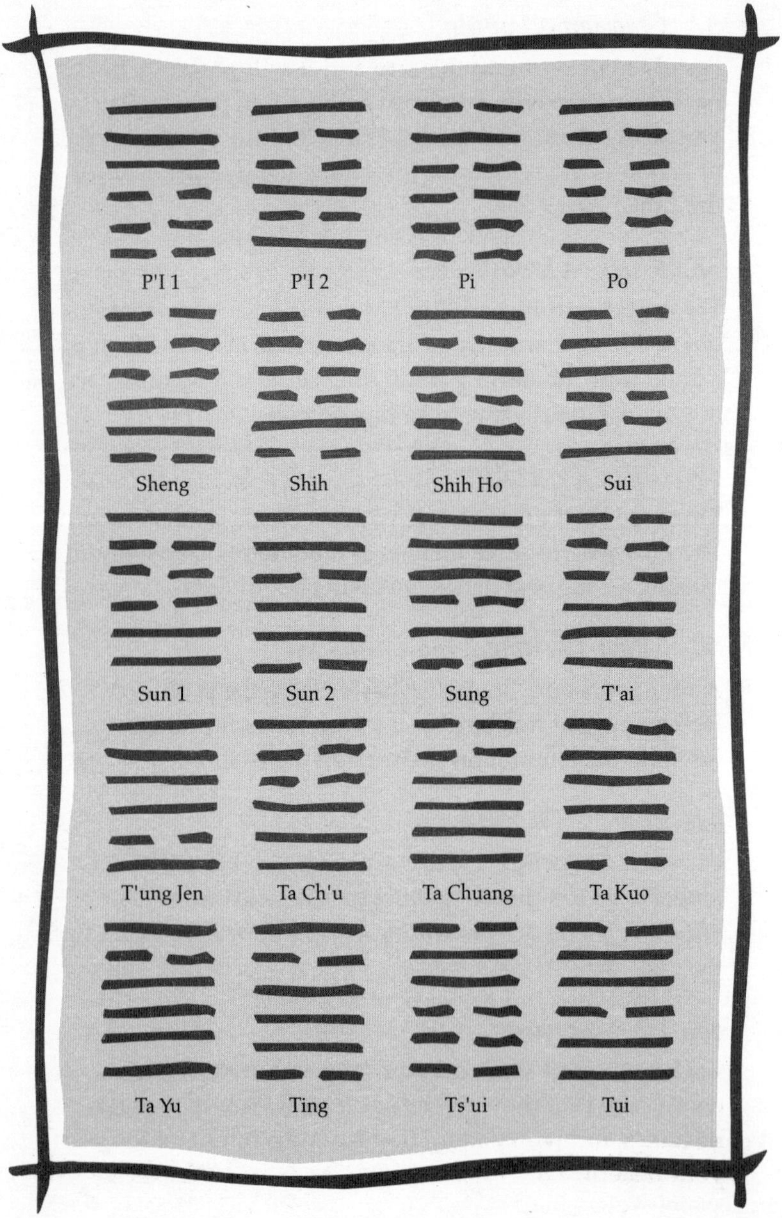

P'I 1

P'I 2

Pi

Po

Sheng

Shih

Shih Ho

Sui

Sun 1

Sun 2

Sung

T'ai

T'ung Jen

Ta Ch'u

Ta Chuang

Ta Kuo

Ta Yu

Ting

Ts'ui

Tui

## 43. Kui – Breakthrough

Take precautions against possible losses and they will be kept to a minimum. Be firm without being pushy and try to cultivate friends, for they will blossom.

## 44. Kou – Meeting

Be resolute: stand your ground and don't give in, whatever you do. Now is not the time to sign contracts or make agreements.

## 45. Ts'ui – Gathering Together

Sincerity and openness will help you to make your relationship especially harmonious now. Keep a guard on your tongue. There may be a bit of a struggle ahead, and if you feel that you are on your own with regard to a project, it is best to ask just one person to help.

## 46. Sheng – Ascending

Be warned that although progress might be on the slow side, at least you are going forwards and are not in reverse. Professional help could be beneficial at the moment, which can generally be regarded as a good time.

## 47. K'un 2 – Repression

Things are probably looking hard, but stay calm, composed and as silent as possible and you will cope, although you may have to dig deep into your reserves and be very determined to do so.

## 48. Ching – The Well

Things are looking up but nothing lasts forever! Insincerity on your part could have disastrous consequences. Excellent judgement regarding a situation or another person may be called for now. It is a time to watch your guard.

## 49. Ko – Change

Big changes regarding opportunities beckon, followed
by a series of smaller ones. Be alert and remember that
sometimes it pays to dress the part. Remember, too, that
material things are not the only ones that matter in life.

## 50. Ting – The Cauldron

You may find that lots of little things conspire to get you
down at the moment: equipment goes wrong, plans run
late. Nothing serious though: life soon picks up and things
start to go well again, heralding further success. Don't
forget to keep the material and spiritual parts of your life
in balance.

## 51. Chen – Thunder

The road ahead is rocky, but stay as calm as you can, it
smoothens out before too long. You may be about to hear
some shocking news, though. Try not to let it affect you
too much – it could be nothing more than tongues wagging.

## 52. Ken – Mountain

If you maintain a low profile, problems that loom may
well pass you by. Avoid taking risks. If you enjoy
meditating, this is a good time for it; if you have never
tried it, this is the best time to start.

## 53. Chien 2 – Growth

'Softly, softly catchee monkey.' A good motto for the time
being. Deal with things as they crop up and don't try to
force the pace whatever you do.

## 54. Kuei Mei – Marrying Maiden

You could have been aiming too high: trim your sails and
you won't regret it. Don't overdo things. And remember
that it's always darkest before the dawn.

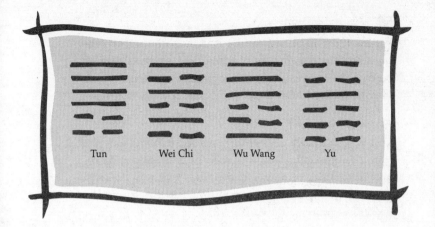

Tun      Wei Chi      Wu Wang      Yu

### 55. Feng – Abundance

Good fortune and good luck beam at you. Worries will soon be a thing of the past – for a time at least.

### 56. Lu 2 – Travel

Movement and moving are on the cards. And with the changes this will bring, long-term commitments should be avoided. This is a time to make friends, but to chose them wisely.

### 57. Sun 2 – Gentle

'Go with the flow', as they say, and be flexible. You could well find that help could come from an unexpected source, so stick to any plans you have made, but do so without sticking your head too far above the parapet.

### 58. Tui – The Joyous

Good news and good fortune come your way. And your behaviour makes people see just how in tune you are with your spiritual side. You could be asked to enter into a partnership: work with the people who make the offer.

## 59. Huan – Dispersal

A time for reason, to take the middle path for any other one could lead to failure of some kind. Friends from the past could resurface: if they do, strong, spiritual bonds may be formed with them.

## 60. Chieh 2 – Restraint

You will probably be feeling shackled in some way, but if you remain calm you will soon be free and ready to take advantage of new opportunities that will present themselves. This is also a good time to work towards becoming more self-aware.

## 61. Chung Fu – Innermost Sincerity

Favoured results should come from properly judged communications. Plans made now for the future will certainly flourish.

## 62. Hsiao Kua – Great Smallness

Success doesn't need to come in one big bag: lots of small packages can be just as rewarding. If you are involved in any legal matters, remember that the devil is in the detail, so read the small print.

## 63. Chi Chi – Completion

Resist the temptation to sit back on your laurels just because you have achieved some success. This is a good time to reinforce the gains you have made and consolidate. Small matters need your attention.

## 64. Wei Chi — Before Completion

Don't make a move until you are certain the time is right, and even then proceed with caution. Think long and hard before getting involved in something new: you could come to regret it later, for there may be things of which you are unaware – important things.

# It's in the numbers

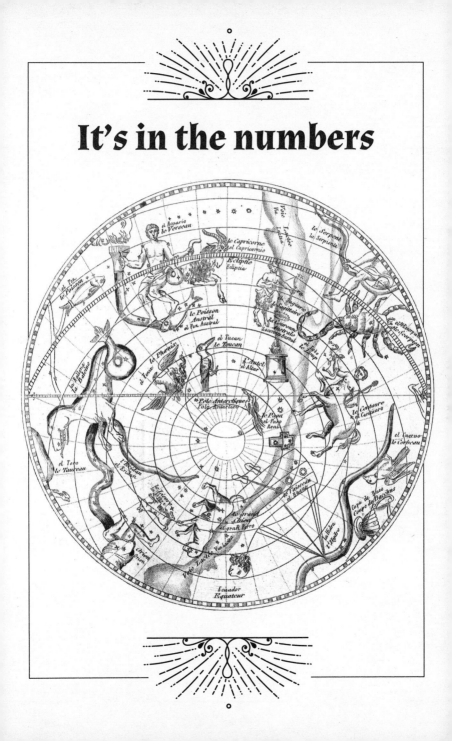

It was Pythagoras, the founder of geometry who asserted that numbers were the essence of all things. Each one, he taught his students at his school at Crotone in Italy, had its own, unique vibration and specific personality. And it was he who divided the human soul into nine different types, the numbers of which are still used today.

There is also a symbiotic connection between numbers and astrology, which has been with us for centuries. Each astrological sign is assigned a planet and a corresponding number, which, it can be assumed, have similar attributes.

For historical reasons, the Sun and the Moon are allocated two numbers because, when the system was devised, there were only seven known planets and nine numbers to be allocated.

Numerology is concerned only with the numbers one to nine, to which all other numbers are reduced. Zero is not a number in numerology terms. It adds nothing at the beginning of a sequence and adds nothing to any other digit to which it is attached. The number ten exists as a composite of the number one $(1 + 0 = 1)$. All subsequent numbers are treated in the same way.

| Star sign | Ruling planet | Number |
| --- | --- | --- |
| Aries | Mars | 9 |
| Taurus | Venus | 6 |
| Gemini | Mercury | 5 |

| Cancer | Moon | 2/7 |
| Leo | Sun | 1/4 |
| Virgo | Mercury | 5 |
| Libra | Venus | 6 |
| Scorpio | Mars | 9 |
| Sagittarius | Jupiter | 3 |
| Capricorn | Saturn | 8 |
| Aquarius | Saturn | 8 |
| Pisces | Jupiter | 3 |

# The Birth Number

This is the number that reveals natural powers and abilities. It is often used as an indication of likely career choices. To calculate this number the individual components of the subject's date of birth are written down and then reduced to a single number. Thus, a person born on 16 November 1945 would have a birth number of 1, calculated as follows:

1 + 6 + 1 + 1 (November is the eleventh month) + 1 + 9 + 4 + 5 = 28.

Being a composite number, 28 is broken down to 2 + 8 = 10

And 10 being a composite number is broken down to 1 + 0 = 1.

The associations of this number with the Sun and the fire signs Leo, Sagittarius and Aries spell leadership. In many religions it is the number of resurrection and being the first number, rising from the chaos of nothing, it is linked with new beginnings, breaks with the past and with limitless energy. It is often linked with assertiveness and masculinity.

People whose birth number is one are often striking to look at, with a mane of fair hair, a lean, athletic body and with beautiful skin that tans glowingly and quickly. They reflect an aura of good health and wellbeing and are usually perceived to be physically attractive with aesthetically pleasing features. The overall impression created by those with this number is one of action, fitness and general good health.

But, being a young number, one can bring with it immaturity and a tendency to sulkiness, especially towards those who spurn attempts to be led. One people need loyalty and when they don't get it, they feel slighted.

Linked to the Moon, now a symbol of femininity, two brings with strong intuition, the power of deep thought and attractive sensitivity. Men with two as their birth number are often closely in touch with their feminine side, and twos of both sexes are often fair skinned with pale, lustreless blonde hair and a dislike of bright sunshine. They may have a slight physique and show a

tendency to underestimate themselves, something that
leads to them having difficulties in standing their ground.

They are often so quietly spoken that one has to strain
to hear what they say. But they have a tendency to say
one thing and do another, something that often causes
difficulties in maintaining relationships.

 A mystical number in many cultures,
as witnessed by the Holy Trinity of the
Christian faith. Chinese philosophers
believed that three was the number
from which creatures that embraced the
Yin and the Yang were created. People
whose birth number is three are usually
uncommonly intelligent and wise: they love life and have
a strong sense of the sensual. The solid physique of
youth can easily give over to fat in middle age, if care is
not taken.

Threes have outgoing personalities and share a dislike
of their own company. They often have psychic abilities
and love acquiring knowledge.

 Another Sun number, which in many
cultures is symbolized by the serpent.
Four people often have a tough,
aggressive nature but keep it hidden
under the well-balanced façade they
present to the world. They enjoy hard
work and the rewards it brings. They
have tough bodies and quick, alert minds, but are often
diffident when it comes to starting relationships because
of a curious lack of confidence. But make friends with a
four and you have a friend for life. That said, remember
the dragon that lurks beneath the surface and be careful
not to stir it.

The number of the planet Mercury, messenger to the gods and child of Maia after whom the fifth month, May, is named. Fives are mentally and physically always on the move. They are often slender of build and find it hard to put on weight, thanks to the effect their constant hurrying and scurrying has on their fast metabolism.

They have persuasive tongues, especially when it comes to sex for they can charm the birds off the trees and whoever they set their sights at into bed. And cheerful extroverts they may be, but they can be anxious and impatient. Also, their incessant movement often disguises prevarication: actually getting things done is quite a different thing from looking busy.

Their agile minds make fives good inventors. Their fertile imaginations make them good authors. Their behaviour may suggest genius: but it might just as easily say madness. That's the trouble with fives. As Bernard Shaw wrote, 'You never can tell, sir, you never can tell.'

Venus's number, six is the symbol of partnership, love and marriage. Those whose birth number it is can be fairly certain that they will enjoy loving and fruitful relationships. Blessed with good figures, their love of the good things in life might lead to a tendency to the sort of plumpness that was once fashionable, but which is now frowned upon in the lean times in which we live.

With their attractive bright eyes, six people have pleasing manners, are outgoing and friendly. But they can also be curiously introverted and enjoy the company of quiet, artistic people. They are home-loving people who enjoy looking good, something that can make them appear overdressed.

There are seven days in the week, seven colours in the rainbow, seven pillars of wisdom, seven branches on the Jewish menorah: seven is perhaps the most magical of the nine single-digit numbers with which numerology is concerned.

Seven people, though, are not so magical by nature (and are often not very tall in stature either). They are realists who are not preoccupied with appearance and superficiality, but instead prefer to cultivate a warm and cheerful disposition.

Sevens are often very friendly and make great company. They enjoy nothing more than seeing others enjoy themselves as much as they do.

With Saturn its associated planet, eight is the number of secret, dark places. It is symbolic of the good aspects of old age – wisdom and patience – and the unfortunate ones – regret, disillusionment and failing health.

People whose birth number is eight are often tall and slender of build. Not that you will notice, for smiling is not something that Saturnine eights are prone to do often.

They mature earlier than their peers, something that makes them liable to express their opinions in an overly forthright way. But the strong ideals that they have and their strong principles often encourage others to seek their advice, something that will be given in the cold, dispassionate way that is typical of the eight person.

Mars, god of war, rules nine, the number of wisdom and virtue – and their opposites – ignorance and profligacy. Nine people often have powerful physiques, ruddy complexions and dark hair. They share a tendency to have facial hair and to have been born with unfortunate birthmarks.

Coming before ten, which reduces to one, nine rekindles the lifespark. This makes nines confident, often overconfident, which is something that can lead to their being impetuous and accident-prone. And while they can be full of vitality and enthusiasm, ambitious and energetic, they can also be insecure and quarrelsome, slapdash and autocratic.

# The Destiny Number

This number shows life's purpose, the opportunities that will present themselves and how they should be used to achieve optimum potential. In calculating the Destiny Number, each letter of the full birth name is ascribed a number. These are then added together and treated as above until a single number is reached.

Thus someone named at birth Michael Mitchell Johnstone would calculate his Destiny Number as follows:

4 + 9 + 3 + 8 + 1 +5 +3 + 4 + 9 + 2 + 3 + 8 + 5 + 3 + 3 + 1 + 6 + 8 + 5 + 1 + 2 + 6 + 5 + 5 = 109 = 1 + 0 + 9 = 10 = 1 + 0 = 1

The name can also be used for more refined readings. By reducing the numerical values of just the vowels of any name to a single numeral we get a number (the Name Vowel Number) that gives an indication that some say represents the Freudian ego – the exposed, conscious outer self. Correspondingly, the Name Consonant Number, calculated using only the numerical values of the consonants, represents the Freudian id – the hidden, unconscious self.

# Name Vowel Numbers

1   Suggests an open, confident personality, but perhaps someone who genuinely believes themselves to be better than their fellows. If this goes unchecked it might lead to selfishness and a tendency to offer the hand of friendship only to fawning acolytes. But ones are a gregarious group, who make friends easily and who enjoy money.

2   Often indicates a lack of self-confidence and a tendency to being perhaps just a little too laid back, but it also hints at great creative talents. If twos can get their act

together, they often make excellent counsellors and caring members of the medical profession.

3     Points to a confident, extrovert nature, to people who enjoy the good things in life so much that they overindulge in them. Those with three as their Name Vowel Number are frank and honest to the point of bluntness. They are natural teachers with a thirst for learning, especially about the arts.

4     Says 'responsibility', 'dependability' and 'stability' but also 'self-doubt'. Four people claim to like freedom in their friendships and their jobs, but deep down they harbour a desire for a more structured existence. Emotionally, they tend to keep themselves to themselves. Professionally, they tend towards careers in the arts, architecture and design.

5     Is often the Name Vowel Number of clever, quick-minded people who enjoy learning languages and acquiring new skills. They may have quick tempers and be obsessive about cleanliness and punctuality. They keep emotional commitments at bay, but love a good gossip.

6     Is a number that suggests a well-balanced nature, perhaps a little reserved and maybe a little over-polite. Those with this number are upset by anything that is controversial, untidy or unjust. They may sit on the fence, seeing both sides of any argument, secretly longing to come down heavily in favour of one side, but holding back from doing so.

7     Encourages a bright, creative nature enjoyed by the sort of person who is always on the go, bouncing here,

there and everywhere, and with a deep desire to please everyone at the same time. They can be intellectual but erratic, often starting ambitious schemes only to drop them when the first hurdle looms.

8    Indicates a conventional nature, someone who is stable and cautious, but with a lively imagination that occasionally shows itself in behaviour that surprises. People with this number don't like sudden change. They are often regarded as plodders, but they usually succeed in getting what they want, and then move on to something else.

9    Is a pugnacious Name Vowel Number, often that of the sort of person who sees things in black and white, with no shades of grey. They act first and think later, but their enthusiasm and generosity often makes those affected by their rash decisions forgive them quickly.

# Name Consonant Numbers

1    Suggests a strong sense of one's own worth and the belief that one's own ideas are always the best on offer.

2    Indicates a prolific imagination and the tendency to live in a fantasy world.

3   Points to a sensual nature and a feeling that one's deeply held religious or psychic beliefs set one apart from one's fellows.

4   Says that a creative nature is married to common-sense but warns that persistence might be mistaken for donkey-like stubbornness.

5   May make those with this number restless and eccentric, which some may find appealing and others unbelievably annoying.

6   is a contemplative number, suggesting a liking for the meditative and the mystical and a dislike of change.

7   Is associated with an instinctive knowledge of how things are and how they should be, and a liking for one's own company.

8   Speaks of caution, an unwillingness to take risks and a dislike of waste. But it also has hints of sexual passion.

9   Is a number of deep desires often unfortunately coupled with an inability to express them, which often leads to dashed ambitions and unrealized dreams.

# It's in the palm of
## your hand

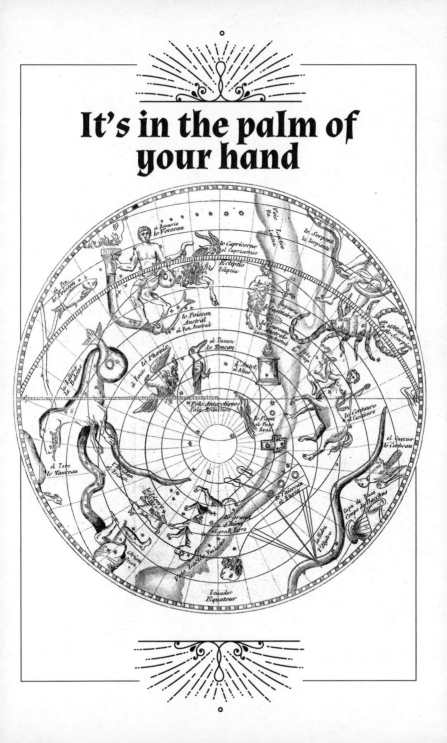

Palmistry is the marriage of two ancient disciplines – chirognomy, which studies what the shape and markings of the human hand, its texture and colour, tell us about the person's character; and chiromancy, which aims to use the information the hand holds to divine future events in life. (Hands can also indicate some diseases: red palms can be a sign of serious liver disease, for instance.)

Like so much of divination, palmistry was first practised in China more than 3,000 years ago (where it was, and remains, part of a larger attempt to see the identity of the 'correct path' by scrutinizing not just the hand but the face and forehead) and in India where it is closely linked to astrology.

Aristotle taught the ancient art of chirosophy (xier = the hand and sophia = wisdom) to Alexander the Great, who at one point had a great part of the civilized world in the palm of his hand.

In AD315, six hundred years after Alexander died, a papal decree threatened excommunication or in extreme cases death, to anyone 'outside the Church', who practised palmistry. It was officially frowned upon during the reign of Henry VIII (r. 1509-47). But had King Henry paid some attention to chirognomy when he was courting Anne Boleyn, he could have been warned of trouble in store, for the young woman was reputed to have an extra finger on her left hand – a sure sign that she was a witch!

As late as during the reign of George IV (r. 1820-30) it was decreed by the British parliament that 'Any person found practising palmistry is hereby deemed a rogue and a vagabond, to be sentenced to one year's imprisonment and to stand in the pillory.'

In Victorian times it came almost to be regarded as a science and was popular in upper-class salons, middle-class parlours and working-class kitchens. Oscar Wilde used palmistry as the theme of one of his stories, *Lord Arthur Saville's Crime*, in which during a party a palm reader tells the young Lord Arthur that it is his destiny that he (Lord Arthur) will commit murder. He does. At the end, driven to distraction by his fate, he kills the man who determined it.

Carl Jung, the famous psychologist, who studied introversion and extroversion, was fascinated by palmistry and his followers came to believe that the outward personality (the extrovert) is in the dominant hand and the inner one (the introvert) in the minor hand. The dominant hand reflects events that have happened and as they are unfolding now – achievements and disappointments, changes of opinion – with the three main lines (heart, head and life) representing the physical organs of the body. The minor hand can give an excellent insight into the subject's potential and what, deep down, they really want in life. In this hand, the heart, head and life lines signify the energies, nervous and sexual, that drive the subject.

Palmistry, like so much of divination, depends on two things – trust between the palmist and the subject, and instinct. The reading should take place in a relaxed atmosphere rather than in a tent at the village fête! A shaded, room fragranced with suitable essential oils is ideal.

An introductory chat can tell the palmist a great deal about the subject: which is the dominant hand; does the subject gesticulate as she talks; are the hands open and relaxed, or are the fingers clenched into a fist; are the fingers adorned with rings. During this time, the reader might take the opportunity of taking the subject's hand in hers, looking at the texture, the colour, the condition of the fingernails and blemishes. And, one of the most important aspects of palmistry – the shape of the hand.

The actual reading can be done by examining the hand physically or by taking a palmprint. Either way, the hands being studied must be washed and thoroughly dried and free of rings.

To make a palmprint (one for each hand) you will need:

1. Acrylic Print-making ink (available from specialist shops).
2. A smooth metal or glass surface on which to roll out the ink.
3. A hard rubber roller (available from specialist shops or photographic supply shops).
4. Glossy paper.

Squeeze some ink onto the smooth surface and push the roller back and forth until it is evenly coated. Roll the roller over the hand to be printed, then position a piece of glossy paper on a soft or rubbery surface and carefully press the hand on to it gently. Now roll the hand off the paper towards the edge, so that the edge of the hand as well as the palm is printed. The subject may need reassuring that the ink comes off easily with soap.

# Types of hands

Just as no two people, not even identical twins, have identical fingerprints, so no two people have exactly the same hands. That said, though, it is possible to identify six basic types of hand that can, in themselves, tell a great deal about the subject of the reading.

## 1. The normal or practical hand

This tends to be on the clumsy side with fingers that are short in comparison with the palm. People with this type of hand often lack patience and are quick to lose their temper. They also tend to be among the most passionate.

## 2. The square or elemental hand

People who have a tendency to being logical and, perhaps, creatures of habit often have square hands. They are also usually very helpful individuals who can be relied on in times of crisis. They are persistent to the point of doggedness, conventional, always above suspicion – and very often boring!

## 3. The spatulate hand

The hand and fingers of this type represent a fan, which indicates restlessness and excitability – the sort of person who can go from one extreme to another in the blink of an eye. Such people are often inventive with an original view of the world that enables them to make discoveries. They are risk-takers and good company, but can be slapdash and have a tendency to bend the rules more than it is wise to do.

## 4. The philosophical hand

These long, bony hands often belong to teachers, philosophers and intellectuals, who are always seeking the truth. The minutiae of life is of little concern to people with Philosophical Hands – they are far too easily distracted. These are people who see the wider picture, often ignoring their immediate surroundings to the point that their untidiness borders on the eccentric.

## 5. The mixed hand

Neither one thing nor the other, this is probably the most difficult to interpret. Sometimes such a hand is clawed, something that indicates long-term anxiety over financial matters, or that the person is over-timid and cautious in everything he or she does.

## 6. The physic or pointed hand

Graceful and conic in shape with pointed, tapering fingers and a long palm, the Physic Hand suggests an intuitive person who is happy to follow his own instincts and is usually quite right to do so.

# All fingers and thumbs

The first thing to look at is the thumb, which represents willpower, and see how it is held naturally. Insecure people tend to curl it up, defensively, within the palm. Then determine its size in proportion to the rest of the hand. When the lower knuckle of the dominant hand's thumb is placed at the bottom of the little finger, it should be about the same length as that finger.

Strong, thick, thumbs say that the sitter has the capacity to deal with whatever life throws in her direction. Long ones indicate rational, clear thinking and leadership qualities. People with short thumbs tend to be subordinate to stronger characters, lacking the will to resist them, which often makes them unhappy. Aggressive tendencies are shown by short stubby thumbs.

More information can be gleaned from the thumb's phalanges (the sections between the joints), which are read from the top down, the first one representing will and the lower one logic. They should be about the same length. If the lower one is longer, then its owner is probably someone who thinks and talks a lot – too much to get down to actually doing anything! If the upper phalange is longer, beware of a person who rushes head first into things and then cries for help as soon as any trouble threatens.

Low self-esteem is indicated by a flattened thumb pad and is something that often manifests itself in sexual promiscuity. A square tip indicates a practical nature, while a spatulate one shows that the owner is especially good with his hands.

The angle of the thumb to the index finger also yields significant information. If it is less than 45° the owner has a tendency to be something of a control freak. An angle of 90° between the two says that the person is a charming extrovert, outgoing and great company. Beware a thumb that curves significantly backwards: it sits in the hand of a killer in every sense of the word.

Each of the fingers is named, as follows. The first (index) finger, Jupiter, indicates ambition and expansion. The second finger, Saturn, is connected with judgement and knowledge. The third (ring) talks of exploits and achievements: it is the finger of Apollo. And the little finger, Mercury, is to do with observation and perception.

Generally, long fingers indicate that the person is something of a perfectionist, and extra-long ones say that he or she is prone to exaggeration. Short fingers indicate an impatient nature.

## The Jupiter finger

A long index finger points to self-confidence and awareness. Its owner is ambitious and more than able enough to achieve these ambitions. A leader, this is a person to whom one can turn during any type of crisis. A medium-length one shows that its owner is confident when confidence is called for, and modest when being such is the order of the day. And whoever has a short index finger is shy, scared of failure, insecure and full of self-doubt.

## The middle finger

A long middle finger talks of ambition without humour. Those with long middle fingers work hard to get ahead, and will surely do so. A medium-length one indicates that the owner has the maturity to know when it is time to work and when it is time to play. A short middle finger is a sign of a careless person who hates routine so much that disorganization is a word often used in his or her connection.

## The ring finger

The finger often associated with creativity, a long one points to an artistic nature that often leads its owner into considering design, especially fashion design, as a career. It can also warn of a gambling streak. One of medium length still points to having a creative nature, but a more traditional, conservative one. A short ring finger means that there is little creativity in its owner's nature.

## The little finger

Length here indicates intelligence and excellent communication skills that make their owners excellent writers and speakers. They might also have a stronger than average sex drive. A little finger that is medium in length says that the owner is of average intelligence – not too bright, but not particularly dim either. And a short one means emotional immaturity and a tendency towards gullibility and naïvety.

# Length

The comparative length of the fingers are also indicative of a person's nature. When the first finger is longer than the ring one, this is indicative of someone who is driven by their ego. Religious leaders and senior officers in the services often have such fingers.

Where the second finger is flanked by index and ring fingers of equal length, the owner has a serious, controlled nature with a well-developed sense of curiosity.

If the third finger is longer than the index finger, then an emotional, intuitive nature is indicated, someone who makes a good doctor or nurse, and whose advice is always well worth listening to.

And if the little finger rises above the top joint of the ring finger, then this is a charismatic person with a quick wit and shrewd business abilities.

# Shape

The shapes of the fingers are also significant. Square ones show a rational, methodical nature, someone who thinks a lot at the expense of creativity. Fingers that are pointed indicate a sensitive nature, fragile daydreamers who are often artists or writers. Someone with conical fingers is usually a person with a flexible nature who often has excellent negotiating skills and to whom emotional security is important, often over-important, to their well-being. People with spatulate fingers can be exhaustingly active not just physically but intellectually: they are innovators and inventors, explorers and extroverts.

## Fingernails

Fingernails, too, play their part in hand-reading. Square ones indicate an easy-going temperament, while broad ones say, 'Beware! I'm a strong character with an explosive temper!' Fan-shaped fingernails are a sign that the owner has been under some sort of stress for quite a long time. A gentle, kind nature is indicated by almond-shaped fingernails, but can say that the person is prone to daydreaming. A selfish, cold personality is shown by narrow nails. Wedge-shaped nails say that the person is oversensitive and as touchy as a nervous cat.

The nails can also indicate health problems. If they are dished, then the person's chemical balance is out of kilter. Dietary deficiencies may result in horizontal ridges forming in the nails: whereas rheumatism may cause vertical ones running down the nails.

## The phalanges

These, the sections between the finger joints are read from the top down. The top one is concerned with introspection, the second corresponds to the subject's attitude to material concerns, and the third with physical desires.

# The major lines of the palm

The lines that criss-cross the palms of the hand are just one of the things that professional palm-readers look at, whereas to the amateurs (and no disrespect to them) who do readings at village fêtes they are very often the only things that are considered. The professional interprets their meaning in conjunction with what we have looked at already, and the other marks that we shall mention later.

Plotting the chronology of the subject's life and assessing whether events have already happened or when they might do so, involves knowing where the lines begin. Horizontal lines should always be read from the thumb side of the hand, and vertical ones from the wrist. Flexibility is the keyword. Remember that in palmistry as in all things concerned with divination nothing is written in stone.

It is impossible to be precise as to where a line starts and where it stops. Lines differ from hand to hand. Some may be stronger in one subject than in another; some may by straight or straighter while others have pronounced curves; some will start at the wrist, others up from it. The line of one hand may stop at one particular mound while the same line on another subject's hand runs through it.

## The life line

This is the line that curves downwards from close to the thumb towards the wrist. The closer to the thumb it starts, then the less vitality the subject is likely to have whereas the wider the curve the greater the energy. A life line that is less well defined than the head line (see below) points to a person who is driven mentally rather than physically.

Chains in the life line are an indication of delicate health, and small lines rising from it denote versatility and physical activity. Lines that seem to swing out of the main one point to a desire to travel and see the world.

Upward hooks along the line after some unfortunate event has been indicated in the reading, suggest that the sitter has made a tremendous effort to get back on her feet after some sort of setback; otherwise they indicate achievement.

Splits along the line point to huge change, conflict perhaps between domestic and professional life, a new job or relationship perhaps.

## The heart line

This is the topmost major line, running horizontally from the side of the hand opposite the thumb. It's the line that reveals relationships, not just romantic ones. If it is almost straight, romance plays little part in the subject's life: he or she views other people in a chilly, rational way. A strongly curved heart line points to the subject who loves being in love and shows it, the sort person who takes the lead in any relationship.

A heart line that curves steeply below the index and middle digits indicates strong sexual desires and passions, not promiscuity, though: that can be shown by a short

1. The life line
2. The heart line
3. The fate line
4. The head line

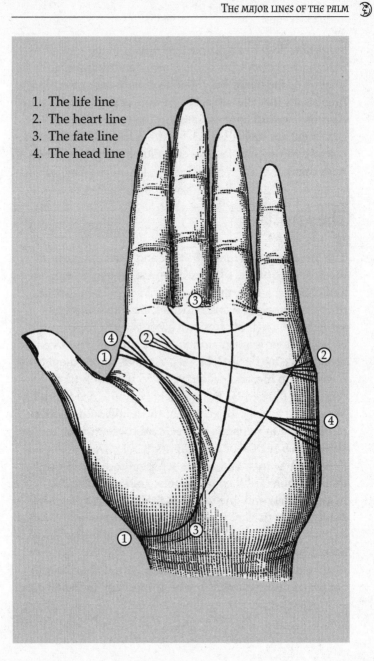

heart line close to the finger and points to the mound of Saturn (see below). Such a line also denotes practicality in matters of the heart. But a line that ends under the middle finger says that the subject is the sort of person who is in constant need of love and reassurance.

If there are lots of branches off the heart line, the sitter enjoys meeting new people and establishing friendships with them.

## The fate line

The line that runs from the wrist and runs upwards towards the mound of Saturn represents career, marriage and children – the practical, central supporting aspects of life. A strong fate line indicates that the subject has settled into life's routines and accepts them happily. If it is not there or is very faint, then the sitter is unsettled and might have to change jobs several times before they make their way in life, and will have to do so with little or no help from the family. But one that begins in the mound of Venus (see below) suggests that the family will interfere, particularly in romantic matters and those relating to the sitter achieving his or her ambitions.

A fate line that almost reaches the middle finger says that the subject will enjoy an active old age. One that begins at the head line suggests that academic effort has played an important part in the subject achieving success in life. One that stops at the heart line is an indication of sexual indiscretion.

An overly thick fate line means a period of anxiety at the time of life indicated by the chronology of the reading.

# The head line

The line running between the life and heart lines. If it
starts off tied to the life line at the start, slavish obedience
to and dependence on other people is indicated. If the
two lines have distinct starting points (which is usual) a
well-balanced, independent nature is indicated.

A long head line points to a person who thinks before
he acts: a short one to someone who is quick-thinking
and incisive. If the line doesn't slant at all, the subject
is likely to be an unsympathetic person lacking in
imagination. A slanting line indicates an imaginative and
intuitive person. A line that curves rather than slants
indicates lateral thinking.

Receptivity to new people is shown by the presence of
lots of outward branches on the head line. If they point
towards the mound of Jupiter (see below) leadership
qualities are suggested. If they point to Saturn, a
hardworking nature is indicated and success in a job
that requires research. Artistic achievement is indicated
by branches that point towards Apollo, and someone
with branches pointing towards the mound of Mercury
should look to a career in the communications industry
or business world. Downward branches suggest periods
of depression, but one that runs to the lunar mound
opposite to the thumb can expect success in the arts
or humanities.

## The triangle and the quadrant

The triangular shape that is often formed by the head,
heart and life lines also has a meaning, as does the area
between the heart and head lines, which is known as
the quadrant.

A wide triangle is an indication of an open person, always willing to take action and with passions that are easily aroused. Meanness of spirit is indicated by a small, cramped triangle.

A wide quadrant is an indication of an impulsive nature that cares little for what the world thinks. But a small quadrant, marked with many lines suggests timidity and fear, someone who is constantly concerned about what people think of them.

# The minor lines

Whereas most of us have the major lines engraved in the palms of our hands, many of us will not have all of the lines that follow – and their absence can be as significant as their presence.

## The success line

Often called the Line of Apollo, the line that runs vertically from the palm towards the ring finger is the line of fame, fortune and success in that which the subject finds important. If it is not there, the subject believes that success can only come through hard work. If there is a break in it, a period of some sort of struggle is indicated.

## The health line

Ideally, the line that on many hands runs up the radial side of the hand, towards the little finger and which is sometimes called the Line of Mercury should not be present, for it indicates an overdeveloped concern for health. One that starts close to the mound of Venus (see below) suggests bad digestion and a long health line on a very lined hand says that worry could cause ulcers.

## The Mars line

Running inside the life line, this is an indication of someone who has vitality with a capital 'V'.

## The via lascivia

A horizontal line that runs across the mound of the Moon (see below) can indicate that the subject suffers from allergies or that an addiction of some sort is causing problems.

## The girdle of Venus

If it is there at all, seen as a semicircle above the heart line and covering the mounds of Saturn and Apollo (see below), it says that the subject is a person of an unusually sensitive nature.

## Travel lines

Running horizontally from the outer side of the hand, below the little finger and lying across the mound of the Moon (see below) in the lower left corner and on the lower Mars mound (see below) these little lines indicate important journeys. And the stronger and longer they are, the more important is the journey.

## Bracelets

These are the horizontal lines between the wrist and the palm. Three of them indicate a long life. If the top one curves and pushes up towards the palm, it could mean that infertility is a problem.

## The bow of intuition

A very unusual line found opposite the thumb, starting at the mound of the Moon (see below) and curving up towards the mound of Mercury (see below), this is an indication of intuition and prophetic ability.

### The ring of Saturn

Another rare line, seen as a small arc below the middle finger, indicating a reclusive nature and tendencies towards miserliness.

### The ring of Solomon

People who are well respected for their common sense often have this line, which runs round the base of the index finger, skirting the mound of Jupiter (see below).

# The mounds

The raised pads on the hands are called 'mounds' or 'mounts' and vary in size and the degree to which they are pronounced. They speak of the subject's character. Running widdershins from the base of the thumb, the mounds are as follows:

## The mound of Venus

Found at the base of the thumb, it is to do with harmony and love. Broad and well-developed, it suggests a strong sex life and a love of all that is sensual, but also a deep love of the family. Sitting high and soft to the touch it is an indication of excitability and fickleness. If it is depressed or

flat, then the subject may by indolent and careless,
but before rushing to criticize, this could be caused by
ill health.

## The mound of Neptune

Sitting at the base of the palm, in the middle of the hand,
the mound of Neptune is often not prominent, but when it
is so and it is well developed, then the subject is probably
a person of some charisma.

## The mound of the Moon

At the bottom of the ulna side of the hand, the mound
of the Moon is related to travel and to the unconscious.
If it is very pronounced, it suggests a person of vivid
imagination but introspective nature, with a tendency
to mendacity.

   Sensitivity and a perceptive nature are indicated by a
normal-sized Moon mound, while those who have a flat
one are probably dull and unimaginative, and unstable
people with a frosty nature.

## Mars lower

Found on the outside edge of the hand above the
mound of the Moon, this represents motivation. If it is
large, though, there is a tendency towards violence and
argument, while a small one may say that the subject is
something of a coward. A normal Mars lower suggests
courage, someone who will pick up the gauntlet and fight
for a cause he believes in.

## The mound of Mercury

Positioned at the base of the little finger, this is the mound of self-expression, of travel and of business abilities. A large one suggests a good sense of humour and a warm, receptive nature. Powers of persuasion, subtlety and quick-thinking are indicated by a normal-size one. But if it is flat, then the subject could well be a bit of a dull loner, shy perhaps or just lazy.

## The mound of Apollo or the Sun

Situated at the base of the ring finger, this has to do with success, charm and creativity. High-achievers in the media, on stage and in sport, often have pronounced mounds of Apollo, but they can be prone to hedonism, extravagance and pretentiousness. An undeveloped one indicates a person who is dull, whose life is aimless and has no interest in culture whatsoever.

## The mound of Saturn

Sitting at the base of the middle finger, this mound if it is over-prominent suggests someone who is gloomy bordering on being reclusive, so intent is he on keeping his head down and earning money. If it is flat or undeveloped, the person is your ordinary man in the street. If the mound merges with Jupiter (see below) it implies someone who is ambitious and serious. And if it merges with the mound of Apollo (see above) then the subject could well be passionate about the arts.

# The mound of Jupiter

This sits at the base of the index finger. Representing how willpower can be used to achieve ambition, this mound, if well-rounded, suggests that its owner is confident that he will succeed. People with large Jupiters like everything to be just so, but they can be generous. If the mound is especially high, then arrogance is a word that is probably associated with the subject. A flat, undeveloped Jupiter is a sign of laziness and selfishness and a dislike of authority.

# Mars upper

In the crease of the thumb, a large Mars upper is a sign of bad temper and cruelty, and a sharp, sarcastic tongue. Moral courage is indicated by a normal Mars upper and cowardliness by a flat one.

# The plain of Mars

Not a mound, obviously, the plain of Mars is in the hollow in the centre of the palm. If the lines around it are distinct and unbroken, the subject probably enjoys good health and prosperity and can look forward to a long life. Optimism is indicated by a flat plain, but should it be hollow, then in all likelihood the subject lacks both drive and ambition.

# Minor marks

As well as using the lines and mounds, diviners can get information from the small marks that many of us carry in the palms of our hands.

## Ascending lines

Branching upwards from the main lines of the hand, these indicate extra energy, and if they continue onwards towards one of the mounds, that mound indicates the realm in which that energy is directed.

## Crosses

Crosses are not a good sign, as they draw out negative aspects of the line on which they are found, although the less distinct the cross is, the less powerful the draw will be. A cross on the mound of Apollo indicates business or financial disappointment whereas one on the mound of Mercury signifies a dishonest personality. Relationships will suffer if there is a cross on Venus. A cross on the mound of the Moon suggests someone prone to self-delusion. But worse of all is a cross that is seen on the mound of Saturn, for it signifies that ambitions will be particularly hard to achieve.

# Descending lines

Just as an ascending line indicates an energy surge, so descending ones point to there being less energy being directed towards the areas governed by the line from which they fork.

# Forked lines

On any of the major lines, forks indicate diversity related to that particular line. Forks on the life line may mean a change in direction at the time indicated by where the fork is. Love affairs or perhaps a change in where the affections lie can be suggested by forks in the heart line. A fork at the end of the fate line points to a successful career bringing fame and fortune. And a fork at the end of the head line is a sign that the subject is a good businessman.

# Grilles

Often found on the mounts of the hand, these little noughts and crosses boards denote obstacles ahead in whatever the mound is associated with. Thus, a grille on Venus suggests greedy lust.

## Islands

Uneven circles on lines and mounds indicate weakness, listlessness and unwelcome change but changes that could lead to better things – eventually. On the life line for example, islands close to the start mean troubled teenage years. On the heart line, they can signify problems with hearing or sight.

## Stars

Something spectacular is in the air when there are stars on the mounds of the hand. On Jupiter (at the base of the index finger) it indicates a good marriage that will enhance career prospects with a consequent boost to finances. On Saturn (base of the middle finger), it suggests that the subject's special talents will bring fame and fortune. On Apollo (base of the ring finger), a star might indicate a major win of some kind or an artistic triumph, whereas a great step forward in knowledge is indicated by a star on Mercury (base of the little finger).

# It's in the stones

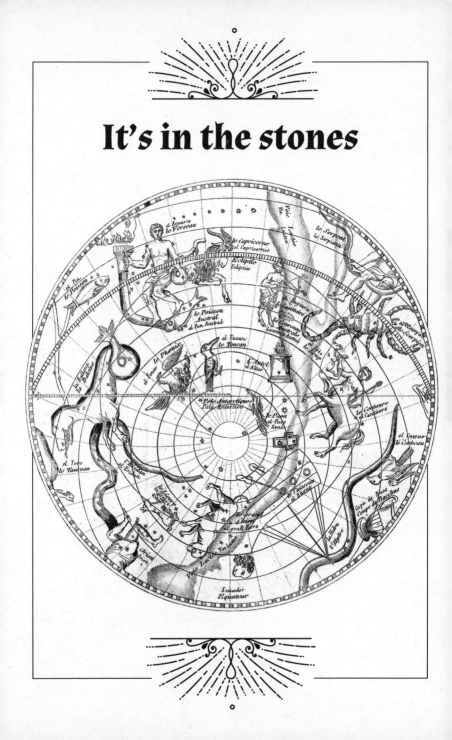

The word 'rune' means secret writing. Casting the runes – stones on which mystic symbols are engraved – began several thousand years ago in Scandinavia, and has its roots in Scandinavian mythology. The symbols represent birds, animals and other things from the world of nature, although their precise meanings are now lost to us.

Runes were dedicated to Odin, the supreme deity in the Scandinavian pantheon, and associated with travel, healing, communication and divination. According to Scandinavian myth, in his search for enlightenment, Odin hung himself upside down on Yggdrasil, the World Tree, and impaled himself on his own spear for nine days. Gazing at the ground, rune stones hidden in Yggdrasil's roots revealed themselves.

The legend probably has its own roots in the mythology of the Volsungr, a tribe of priest-magicians and guardians of the ancient forests, who used an early form of runes (Ur Runes) to divine the future. At the end of the last Ice Age, the Volsungr spread south, bringing their knowledge with them. Later, they retreated back whence they came, but by then runic divination had spread throughout Scandinavia and into central Europe.

By Roman times, the runes had evolved into Futhark, a runic alphabet. Interpreting the meaning of the stones was a mystery granted only to a few. The Roman historian Tacitus writing in *Germania* described a runic ceremony during which a branch was cut from a nut-bearing tree and cut into small pieces (rune slips) on which runic symbols were marked. These were cast on a white cloth and interpreted by a priest.

Whenever a journey had to be made the runes were cast to establish the most propitious time to set out, and so the runes followed the trade routes, across Europe and into Mediterranean lands. The Vikings took them from Iceland to America, to Russia, Turkey, Greece and even North Africa as evidenced by the runic carvings found on monuments and other artefacts.

In Anglo-Saxon England, kings and bishops had the power to read the runes, but the practice gradually died out, not just in Britain but in other parts of the world where Christianity (which regarded the use of runes as pagan) was taking hold. Some people continued to cast them, and some people continued to believe what they said, but just as people who read the future through other means often came to be regarded as harmless eccentrics at best, dangerous heretics at worst, so casting the runes was sidelined to be something of a 'party trick'.

Interest in them was renewed during the rise of German nationalism in the nineteenth and twentieth centuries, when there was a revival of interest in Teutonic folklore, fuelled in no small part by Wagnerian operas. However, when this revival came to be intricately linked with Nazism, the runes once again fell into disfavour.

But with the renaissance of the 'New Age', runes have once again become popular, not just for divining the future and for increasing one's knowledge of oneself but to be carried as talismans, each sign having its own association.

The runes that are popularly used today are the Germanic Futhark set, which is divided into three sets ('*aettirs*') of eight runes each, making twenty-four in all. Each of these aettirs is named after a Norse deity. The first eight are dedicated to Freya, the goddess of love and lust, war and death; Hagal, the guardian of the other gods and goddess in the Norse pantheon, presides over the second set; and Tiwaz, god of justice and law, of war and of the sky rules the third aettir.

The qualities of these three gods influence the runes in the aettir dedicated to them, each rune having a double meaning – a material one and a spiritual one. Nine of them read the same whichever way they are looked at. The others can be drawn upright or reversed. But any of the runes may appear as a 'merkstave' (which literally means 'dark stick' and implies a 'dark' meaning), depending on how the runes are cast. Note that a 'reversed' or 'merkstave' meaning is not the opposite of its primary meaning, but usually has a more negative connotation.

Runes can help you to look deeply into the inner self, pinpointing fears and desires and highlighting the hidden factors that will shape the future. They describe the positive and negative influences, pointing out ways to use the former and overcome the latter, and to make constructive choices for the future.

The way in which the runes can be interpreted is given below. Being of such antiquity, there are variations in the names of each of them. We give the two most commonly used names for each symbol along with the literal runic meaning and the facet of life with which it is most intimately associated.

# Freya's Aettir

### Fehu/Feoh (Cattle = possessions and prosperity)

This is a sign of prosperity and material gain, probably from past efforts being rewarded. It signifies foresight and fertility and as an energetic rune, it speaks of new opportunities and social success. Reversed or merkstave it signifies that what has been achieved, either tangible or intangible such as self-esteem may be lost: it also indicates failure, perhaps brought about by greed or stupidity. As a talisman, Fehu is good for achieving a goal, gaining promotion or to bring luck to a new business.

### Uruz/Ur (Bison = strength)

A rune of strength, courage and overcoming obstacles, the right way up it can indicate that what seemed to have been a loss, is in fact an opportunity in disguise. It speaks of action and good health, and promises wisdom and the chance to gain a deeper insight into oneself. Reversed or merkstave, it suggests a character that is too easily led or influenced by others, something that can lead the subject into the land of lost opportunity. Drawn this way it also threatens ill health and inconsistency, ignorance and callousness, brutality and violence. Anyone seeking a surge in sexual potency or a stronger will, should wear Ur as a talisman.

### Thurisaz/Thorn (Thorn = challenge or protection)

Drawn or falling the right way up Thurisaz suggests change of some sort and is also concerned with male sexuality and fertility. It can indicate the approach of a destructive force or conflict, but one that will be seen off if instincts are listened to and followed. Merkstave or reversed, Thurisaz warns of vulnerability leading to some sort of danger. It whispers of betrayal and its approach, perhaps in the shape of a malicious person with evil in their heart. Wear this rune as a talisman if seeking help in study or meditation, or the resolution of an unfortunate situation.

### Ansuz/Oss (A god = communication)

An increased awareness of what the future holds is heralded when Ansuz appears. With its direct association with Odin, this is a rune of inspiration, wisdom, aspirations and communication. It promises spiritual renewal and progress, clear vision and good health. Appearing the wrong way, Ansuz implies that manipulative, selfish people will bring misunderstanding in their wake, which will lead to a feeling of disillusionment. It also warns to be on guard lest vanity and pomposity rear their ugly heads to the detriment of the subject. As a talisman it helps in divination and in making wise decisions, it is also useful if the wearer seeks leadership.

### Raido/Rit (Riding = action)

An indication of travel in all its many guises, be it physical such as a holiday or a change of location, a change of lifestyle, or perhaps an indication of a spiritual journey as the soul moves towards its destiny. It offers the chance to put things in perspective. Drawn merkstave or reversed, Raido suggests that a crisis of some sort is brewing or that injustice and irrationality will threaten disruption, bringing delusion in its wake. It can also suggest that the querent feels caged in by present circumstances. As a talisman it protects travellers, brings change and eases unfortunate situations, particularly if a reconnection of some sort is being looked for.

### Kano/Kenaz/Kaon (Torch = inner wisdom)

This is a rune of the inner voice and inner strength, of guidance and illumination. It promises that light will be cast into the dark places, bringing regeneration in its glow. It promises the ability to create new realities that bring with them hope and invigorating strength. Face down or reversed though, it stifles creativity and says that illness and negative influences – dissolution, hopelessness, mendacity and despair – will cloud life in the immediate future. Wear or carry a Kenaz rune as a talisman to dispel anxiety and fear, for inspiration and creativity.

### Gebo/Gifu (Gift = partnership)

Generosity is the word that is often associated with Gebo, which relates to all kinds of exchanges including contracts, love, marriage and sexual congress. Gebo promises balance and equality. It is a rune that cannot appear reversed, but if it is cast merkstave, then greed and loneliness will cast their shadows causing spiritual and emotional emptiness. Gebo is an excellent talisman to strengthen a relationship and to bring luck and fertility.

### Wunjo/Wunna (Joy = pleasure)

Bringing comfort, joy and pleasure in its wake, along with the promise of prosperity, good fellowship and harmony, Wunjo also warns of the dangers of going to extremes. But if a little self-control is exercised, then the querent will benefit from their true worth being recognized. When it appears the wrong way, Wunjo warns of sorrow and strife, and of being alienated. It whispers of delays, of the dangers of drinking too much, and of being possessed by uncontrollable rages. Worn as a talisman, Wunjo helps to motivate and to bring unfinished tasks to successful conclusion.

# Hagal's Aettir

### Hagalaz/Hagal (Chaos = change and destruction)

Hagalaz, the Mother Rune, indicates uncontrolled forces wreaking havoc, disrupting plans and ushering a time of trials and tests. But all is not lost, for Hagal also suggests that the crises will lead to completion or closure of some sort that heralds an inner harmony. Merkstave (it cannot be reversed) it says that a catastrophic natural disaster may be about to strike. And on a personal level it indicates loss of power and a period of stagnation, hardship and loss, brought about perhaps by ill health. As a talisman, Hagalaz removes unwanted influences and what appears to be a circle of never-ending destruction.

### Naudhiz/Naut/Nyd (Need = constraint)

Representing needs that can be met by reacting positively to deprivation, Naudhiz says that conflict can be overcome by willpower, that delays and restriction can be endured (and have to be) and that fears have to be faced. Reversed or merkstave it suggests that freedom will be restricted and that self-control is essential as poverty and deprivation beckon. It also hints at emotional hunger. Wear it as a talisman if there is a need that has to be fulfilled, or to turn a negative fate into a positive one.

### Isa/Is (Ice = standstill or stillness)

Another rune that is irreversible, this is a reinforcing rune, underlining the message of those around it. It talks of challenging frustrations, that creativity is being blocked by psychological forces, and that this time of standstill is a time to look inwards and wait for clarity to appear. Merkstave it is a ghastly rune, presaging treachery and deceit, and warning the querent to beware of being ambushed by the plotting of others. As a talisman it can be worn to give breathing space or to bring something to an end.

### Jera/Yer (Year = harvest and life cycles)

This is the rune of the harvest, when the results of previous efforts can be gathered in. It heralds in a happy period of peace. Jera also says that a breakthrough of some sort will bring a period when things have become stagnant. Merkstave (Jera can't be reversed) it warns of an unexpected reversal of fortune which may mean a major change in life. Conflict becomes unavoidable, poverty beckons and timing goes awry. Wear it as a talisman to encourage change and fertility.

### Eiwaz/Yr (Yew = endings and mysteries)

The yew tree represents the cycle of death and rebirth and when Eiwaz appears, natural endings leading to new beginnings are suggested. Changes and turning points, maybe brought about by fears being confronted, lie around the corner. Merkstave, it warns of confusion and destruction, and an inability to get round something that is blocking the way. As a talisman it can bring about huge changes or show the way around huge difficulties.

### Perthro/Peorth (Dice cup = initiation, the essence of one's being)

A rune that says that deep transformative powers are at work, this is the rune of what has yet to be revealed and the rune of taking chances. It can indicate mystery and secrecy and psychic abilities. Merkstave it warns of harmful addiction and stagnation, bringing with it an inability to understand others and a sense of finality. As a talisman it helps divination and enhances psychic powers. Pregnant women often wear or carry Perthro as it is believed it eases the pain of childbirth.

### Algiz/Aquizi (Elk-sledge = protection)

This is often regarded as one of the most difficult runes to interpret. It suggests that help will come from an unexpected quarter to ward off a threat of some kind. Algiz also offers a connection to the powers in whose hands lies our fate and encourages us to channel our energies towards the greater good. Reversed, it is a sign that hidden dangers lie ahead, ill health may be about to strike and a warning to consider any advice from a third party before acting on it. Algiz protects as a talisman and helps build defences.

### Sowilo/Sig (Sun = wholeness and potential)

The rune of potential and success, energy and expansion, Sowilo promises that goals will be achieved and honour bestowed. It presages a union between the conscious and the unconscious: but it also counsels restraint. Merkstave it speaks of bad advice leading to false goals being set, of despair and of retribution. Sowilo, as a talisman, gives a boost to energy levels, increases strength, and generally encourages enthusiasm.

# Tiwaz's Aettir

### Tiwaz/Tiu (Star = justice and victory)

Honour, justice, leadership and authority are words that are commonly associated with Tiwaz. The rune says that the questioner knows where his true strengths lie and points to a willingness to self-sacrifice. It predicts victory and success in a competition that is on the horizon, or in a legal matter in which the subject is involved. Reversed or merkstave, it suggests a reversal in energies and creative flow. It hints that the querent suffers from metal stagnation, that he or she is over-analytical and prone to self-sacrifice. Justice and imbalance often appear in the wake of Tiwaz reversed, along with strife, war and conflict, a failure in competition and if all that wasn't bad enough, dwindling passion, difficulties in communication and perhaps a separation of some sort. As a talisman, Tiwaz protects the material surroundings, brings victory, strengthens will and can help heal wounds.

### Berkano/Birca (Birch = rebirth)

Berkano is the rune of birth, general fertility, mental, physical and personal growth and liberation. Berkano brings the light of spring with it, promising new growth and new beginnings. A meeting might be heralded that will bring with it arousal and desire. Berkano also promises that an enterprise or new venture that has already begun will be successful and bring prosperity. Reversed or merkstave is a warning of family problems and domestic troubles and that someone close to the querent is causing anxiety. If this rune is cast the wrong way, beware of carelessness and loss of control, a blurred consciousness, deceit, sterility and stagnation. As a talisman Berkano can be used for healing infections, to bring about a good harvest and to make a fresh start.

### Ehwaz/Eh (Horse = harmony)

Transportation of some kind – a horse, a car, plane, boat or any other means of transport – is indicated when Ehwaz appears. It heralds change, and change for the better, brought about by gradual development and steady progress. The rune promises harmony and teamwork, trust and loyalty. If a marriage is in the offing when Ehwaz appears it will be an ideal one. It also confirms beyond any doubt the meaning of the runes around it in a reading. Reversed or merkstave is not necessarily a bad sign, rather it suggests a craving for a change of some sort, a restlessness or being confined in a situation not of the subject's own making. But it can also presage reckless haste, disharmony, mistrust and betrayal. Wear Ehwaz as a talisman to bring power, for communication purposes and, if the querent is a believer in Wicca or witchcraft, Ehwaz is the runic talisman that best helps to deliver it.

### Mannaz/Man (Man = the self, humanity and tradition)

Mannaz talks of the subject's attitude towards other people and their attitude towards the subject, it mentions friends and enemies, and social order. Mannaz is concerned with intelligence, forethought and creative skills and abilities. When the rune appears the querent can expect to receive some sort of aid or cooperation. Reversed or merkstave is a warning of depression, mortality, blindness and self-delusion. And if that wasn't bad enough, it also says beware of cunning, slyness, manipulation and that no matter where help is looked for, it won't be found. A Mannaz rune can be worn as a talisman to represent someone else or a group of people, and to establish social relationships.

### Laguz/Lagu (Water = life forces and emotions)

Laguz is a rune of the sea, of water's ebb and flow and of the healing power of renewal. It emphasizes imagination and psychic matters, dreams and fantasies, the mysteries of the unknown. It hints at the importance of what is hidden or belongs to the underworld. Reversed or merkstave, Laguz is an indication of a period of confusion in the subject's life and that he may be making wrong decisions through lack of proper judgement. He may be suffering from a lack of creativity or scared that he is in a rut. At its worst, a reversed or merkstave Laguz presages insanity and obsession, and being cast into such deep despair that unspeakable thoughts come to mind. As a talisman, Laguz enhances psychic abilities and helps those who wear or carry it to face up to their fears. It stabilizes emotional disorders and helps uncover what is hidden.

### Ingwaz/Ing (The earth god = people)

Ingwaz is concerned with male fertility, gestation and internal growth. It is all about common sense and simple strengths, the home and love of the family, caring and human warmth. It presages a period of rest and relaxation, when anxieties disappear, loose strings are tied and querents find themselves free to move in new directions. Irreversible, if Ingwaz appears merkstave, it brings impotence, movement without change and hard work that brings little reward. Wear Ingwaz as a talisman to bring fertility and growth or to encourage good health and restore balance if it has gone walkabout.

### *Othala/Odal (Homestead = ancestral property)*

A rune of possessions, house and home, and what the subject holds to be truly important in her life. It is also a rune of groups, promising group order and prosperity. It is, too, concerned with homelands and spiritual heritage, experience and fundamental values. It promises aid in spiritual and physical journeys. It is a source of safety and of abundance. Reversed or merkstave it forewarns of customary order and totalitarianism. It promises bad karma, prejudice and narrow-minded provincialism. As a talisman, Othala helps the wearer to acquire property, to bring a project to a successful conclusion and to strengthen family ties.

### *Dagaz/Dag (Day = integration)*

Dagaz suggests the dawning of breakthrough, awareness and awakening. It promises that clarity will light up the subject's life and says that now is the time to embark on a new enterprise. When Dagaz is drawn up, the subject is being told that using one's will can bring about desired change. It talks of security and certainty, growth and release. Merkstave (it cannot be reversed), it is not a particularly bad sign, presaging completion and ending, although at worst it can say that hope is about to be lost. Dagaz, as a talisman, brings a positive outcome to any situation that concerns the carrier.

Modern rune sets often contain a blank one. Being an invention of the 1980s, there is no historical support for this and it should not be used by anyone who takes the runes seriously. But, those who do use it refer to it as Wyrd and interpret it as a sign that all possibilities are open: that life is what you make it, although it does acknowledge outside influences that are beyond the subject's control. Being blank, it cannot be cast reversed or merkstave.

Traditionalists also scorn the use of rune cards – the term is hopefully self-explanatory – but they are convenient and can be slipped into a handbag or pocket more easily than a bag containing twenty-four stones. They can also be used more discreetly when a question arises suddenly, and a believer wishes to consult the runes to find the answer.

Both cards and stones are readily available at specialist shops. Some people prefer to make their own, and do so with appropriate ceremony. Whichever, the runes should be kept in a special bag, velvet or silk is best, and perhaps of a colour with which the user has special associations.

# Runic spreads

There are several spreads that can be used to divine the future by casting the runes. The twelve-rune circle is one that is often used, as is the nine-stone sacred grid and the cross. Many commercially available rune sets come with instructions on these and other ways of using them, which are often based on Tarot spreads.

But perhaps the simplest (and simplicity is often the most effective) is the three-rune spread whereby the querent focuses on the question to be answered and casts three runes. The first one indicates the situation, the second the action required and the third reveals the outcome. Once the various symbols, their meanings and the variations that result in a rune being drawn merkstave, have been understood, it is not too difficult to use the runes to help find the answer to any question.

# It's in the stars

# 'The fault, dear Brutus, is not in our stars. But in ourselves...'

**C**assius's words to Brutus in Shakespeare's *Tragedy of Julius Caesar* suggest that the noble conspirator had little belief in astrology. Not of course, that Shakespeare would have known, but it would have been strange if the Roman assassin had not believed that the stars had some influence on the course of events, for by 44BC, the year when Caesar was murdered, astrology had been an accepted part of life for many centuries.

In essence, astrology is the study of how the Sun, Moon, planets and stars are related to life on Earth. It is based on the belief that these heavenly bodies form patterns that reveal a person's character or future. In addition to its influence on individuals, astrology has been and still is applied over wider areas. Comets, eclipses of the Sun and Moon and other unusual astronomical events have been taken as portents of war and calamities.

Although very early agricultural societies – in Babylon, Egypt (particularly in Egypt) and China – linked the regular movements of the Sun, planets and stars to the seasons, the rains and the growth cycles of their crops, the principles on which modern astrology is based were laid down around 4,000 years ago in Babylon, present-day southeastern Iraq.

With the development of mathematics, the Babylonians were able to prepare refined astrological observations and calendars, much more sophisticated than anything available to the Ancient Egyptians and their contemporaries in other parts of the world. Not surprisingly, therefore, early astrology was strongly linked with astronomy and religion. The link with astronomy persisted until the time of Tycho Brahe and Johannes Kepler in the sixteenth century. And whereas astronomy, in the West at any rate, is regarded as a science, astrology has come to be regarded as a divinatory art that sceptics call pseudo-science.

To the Babylonian astrologers, the movements of the heavenly bodies were linked to a complex mythology, which, somewhat modified, became the basis of astrological interpretations in the West. The Babylonians' astronomical and astrological studies were preserved and developed by the Greeks and the Arabs and astrology was popular in the Europe of the Roman Empire. However, it fell from favour with the coming of Christianity, as people sought guidance from religious leaders rather than astrologers.

But from the eleventh century onwards astrology found itself back in favour, with many monarchs employing their own royal astrologers. Among these sages was Nostradamus, the court physician to Charles IX of France. His prophecies, many based on astrology, were published in 1555 and still sell today, especially in times of crisis. Not only is he believed by his admirers to have predicted the First and Second World Wars, he is said to have foreseen the rise of the Kennedy clan in the United States, and even the events of 9/11.

Interestingly, but perhaps not surprisingly, astrology was also developing on the other side of the world. When the Spanish conquistadors conquered Mexico and Guatemala in the early sixteenth century, among the writings they found were several astronomical treatises dating from a thousand years before, drawn up by the

Mayans who developed astrological systems linked to astronomical observations and a highly accurate calendrical system.

There are two main types of astrology in use around the world. In the first, a chart is drawn up according to the time of birth of the person whose horoscope is being cast. In the second, the chart is cast for a precise moment when a question is to be asked by the subject and answered by the horoscope.

Sidereal astrology (which takes into account the position of the stars) is used mainly in the East and Vedic astrology. Its fatalistic, karmic approach is popular in India and the rest of the subcontinent.

# Astrological conceits

Underlying astrological concepts is the image of the Zodiac, a band of constellations lying in the apparent paths of the Sun, Moon and the planets. The Zodiac is divided into twelve equal parts called signs. Each of the signs has certain characteristics, which are determined by a particular planet and other factors. Astrologers believe that the signs determine how the planets affect a person's character.

The Zodiac was originally developed by the Ancient Egyptians and refined by the Babylonians, Greeks and Romans whose names for the planets and signs of the

Zodiac are those we use today. Some of these names refer back to the Babylonians. For example, the heaviest rainfall (not that it was all that heavy) occurred in Babylon when the Sun was in a certain constellation. As a result, astrologers came to call that constellation Aquarius, the water bearer, a name that western astrology still uses today. Others are called after mythological animals: Cancer the Crab, Leo the Lion and so on. A different set of Zodiacal animals is used as a basis of Chinese astrology, which is best known in Japan, Korea and Southeast Asia.

Astrologers place the Earth at the centre of things. They adopt this conceit to enable them to determine the positions of the heavenly bodies in relation to the Earth, believing that studying these positions can reveal a person's character and future. Around the Earth, revolve the planets, which for astrological purposes include the Sun and the Moon. (Until 1781, when William Herschel announced the discovery of Uranus, astrologers knew of just six planets – Venus, Mercury, the Earth, Mars, Saturn and Jupiter.) Each planet is ascribed a force that affects a person in its own, particular way. Astrologers believe that the planets influence a person more than any other aspect of astrology.

Astrologers divide the Earth's surface into twelve houses, each of which presents certain characteristics of an individual's life. They also hold that the houses determine how the planets influence a person's daily life.

# The future charted out

Armed with knowledge of the constellations and the position of the planets in them at any time, astrologers draw up their horoscopes, charts that show the relative position of the Sun, Moon, stars and planets at a given time. Horoscopes can be prepared as a birth chart for an individual or a more general chart assessing the influence of the planets and stars on daily life.

To draw up a birth chart the astrologer needs to know the exact time (Greenwich Mean Time) and date of birth. All astrologers worth their salt will have a set of Ephemeris tables, which show the position of the planets within each constellation for as far back as needs be. Each of the twelve signs is believed by astrologers to be associated with definite aspects of character – temperament, physiology and other attributes. In establishing the relative positions of the heavenly bodies in their charts, astrologers claim to be able to predict the future of the subject and advise him or her of paths to follow or actions or decisions to make.

More general horoscopes can be cast for all those born under a particular sign for any period – day, week, month and year – and these are the horoscopes that most of us read in out morning papers or glossy magazines. Newspapers began publishing them, in England, in the 1930s and it wasn't long before they spread to other countries.

Interest in astrology has increased since then and today, with many more people seeking to live their lives in tune with the natural rhythms and cycles of nature, with their minds open to new horizons, astrology is more widely followed than ever before.

# A little basic information

It takes one year for the Earth to revolve around the Sun, and in doing so it follows an elliptical path. (At one time it was thought that its path was perfectly circular, but in 1609, Johann Kepler showed that this was not the case.) Between the two are Venus and Mercury. All the other planets – Mars, Jupiter, Saturn, Uranus and Neptune, and the dwarf planet Pluto – are farther from the Sun than the Earth.

Astrologers divide the circle of the elliptic into twelve equal sections of 30 degrees each. The first starts at the point where the Earth's equator, projected into space, crosses the plane of the elliptical on 21 March – the Vernal or Spring Equinox. This is the first day of Aries, the first sign of the Zodiac. Each of the sections is allocated one of the Zodiac signs. People born under each sign are ascribed the characteristics identified with their sign, something we shall come to later.

The twelve signs represent the natural cycle of the year. The first six signs span spring and summer, the sunshine-

filled months of birth and growth to maturity, when
the countryside is clothed in green and, in the northern
hemisphere we sow our crops and, later, harvest them.
When Virgo gives way to Libra, things change: the Sun
loses its warmth, our fields lie brown and empty and our
lives seem similarly dull and lacklustre. But with Pisces,
the smell of change is in the air. Rebirth is around the
corner. The wheel has turned full cycle.

The signs are:

| | |
|---|---|
| Aries, the ram | 21 March – 20 April |
| Taurus, the bull | 21 April – 21 May |
| Gemini, the twins | 22 May – 21 June |
| Cancer, the crab | 22 June – 23 July |
| Leo, the lion | 24 July – 23 August |
| Virgo, the virgin | 24 August – 23 September |
| Libra, the scales | 24 September – 23 October |
| Scorpio, the scorpion | 24 October – 22 November |
| Sagittarius, the archer | 23 November – 21 December |
| Capricorn, the goat | 22 December – 20 January |
| Aquarius, the water bearer | 21 January – 19 February |
| Pisces, the fish | 20 February – 20 March |

(These are the generally accepted dates: but they may
differ by a day.)

To prepare a horoscope, which is based on the positions
of the planets in the Zodiac signs and houses, a horizontal
line is drawn across the centre of a circle. The line
represents the horizon: the planets that are above the
horizon at the time the horoscope is being prepared will be
drawn above the line, the others below it.

The houses are marked around the edge of an inner circle,
the first one being immediately below the horizon line on

the left of the circle and proceeding anticlockwise so that the twelfth house is immediately above the first. The Zodiac signs, the positions of which vary according to the time and year, are marked around the circumference of the outer circle. The position of the planets is marked in the space between the two. By referring to various tables, astrologers can position each of them in its respective constellation, and each constellation in its respective house for the date required and then analyze the chart and give their reading.

It is not possible in the confines of a book such as this to detail every aspect of the horoscope and what each one means. The variations are too many and too detailed to allow that. But thanks to modern technology, having a personal birth chart drawn up is no longer the preserve of the rich and royal as it was in times gone by. There are several excellent websites from where, usually for a fee, a personal chart can be obtained. All the enquiring reader has to do is refer to a decent search engine, key in the appropriate words and a range of options will appear.

# The planets

Each sign of the Zodiac is ruled by one of the planets, each of which controls an aspect or aspects of our lives. The Ancients, believing that the Earth was at the centre of things, thought there were five planets. When it was realized that the Earth was a planet, astrologers disregarded this, and decided to keep our planet at the centre of things. But when in 1781, William Herschel sighted Uranus, in 1846 when Johanne Galle discovered the existence of Neptune and in 1930 when Pluto floated into the ken of American astronomer Clyde Tombaugh, astronomers were forced to reconsider things. These three planets have now been assimilated into present-day astrology, but things may have to change again, if, as some astronomers believe there is a tenth planet. It is, some say, the only way to explain Pluto's eccentric orbital path.

*Jupiter*, the supreme god in the Roman pantheon, tells us of our need for expansion, abundance and wisdom. It is concerned with what we believe in and the philosophies that colour our lives. Being an expansive planet, it is also linked with excess.

*Mars*, named after the god of war, is the planet most concerned with the way we assert ourselves and what it is that drives us. It powers our activities and energies.

*Mercury*, the messenger god, tells us about our intellects and the way in which we express our ideas. It is also connected to our siblings and our relationships with them.

*The Moon* and our emotional nature go hand in hand. It influences the type of nurturing we need from our mothers to make us complete, well-rounded people. It is also influences how we relate to others.

*Neptune*, the Roman god of the sea, demonstrates our need to be at one with the rest of humanity. It shows us how to be compassionate and complete, but it encourages a grey area between fantasy and reality and makes it difficult for us to distinguish between the two.

*Pluto*, the Roman ruler of the infernal regions, is the orb that tells us transformation is possible, pointing us in the direction in which we can experience regeneration and showing how we can achieve it. It has, astronomically speaking, been downgraded to a dwarf-planet.

*Saturn*, the Roman deity who devoured all but three of his children, controls our ambitions, the way we accept (or don't accept) our responsibilities and the very structure of our lives. In indicating our ability to order out talents, it forces us to take stock of our assets and liabilities.

*Uranus* is the personification of the Greek heaven. Brilliant Uranus loves the original and the unconventional, whether it be astonishing invention or acts of wilful rebellion.

*Venus*, named in honour of the goddess of love, is said to be concerned with our relationships and the choices we make in life, both personal and material. It influences the decisions we make, especially when it comes to choosing the things and people we value.

# The houses

Everything in astrology has its own particular significance, especially the position of the planets in the various houses. By knowing the associations that each planet has, and marrying these with the aspects of our lives with which the houses are connected, astrologers can tell us much about ourselves. For example, knowing that Jupiter is connected with wisdom and the fifth house with self-expression, children, identity, security and play, a professional astrologer was able to say to someone born in Edinburgh at 16.10 on 16 November 1945 (the author), 'your happy and expansive childhood laid the foundations for a trusting attitude in life'. He went on, 'You may be unreceptive to other people's opinions or oversensitive when your own opinions are challenged.' Both of which (and much of the rest of the horoscope) were too remarkably accurate!

| House | Concerns |
| --- | --- |
| First | Self-absorption, personal projection and appearance. |
| Second | Values, self-worth, finances and assets, and security. |
| Third | Travel, local network, siblings and communications. |
| Fourth | Foundations, family, ancestors and home atmosphere. |
| Fifth | Self-expression, children, identity, security and play. |
| Sixth | Service, working environment, health and integration. |
| Seventh | Partnership, dealings with others and adversaries. |
| Eighth | Other resources, inheritance, secret powers and death. |
| Ninth | Long-distance travel, higher education and the law. |
| Tenth | Ambitions, authorities, goals and professional expression. |
| Eleventh | Social affinities, groups, friendships and political visions. |
| Twelfth | Withdrawal, isolation, the divine and inner worlds. |

# The Sun signs

The position of the Sun in the sky is the easiest astrological observation to make. This is because throughout the year, the Sun moves approximately one degree each day, and so it is possible to be precise about its position at any given date. It was this ease that made it possible for newspapers in the 1930s to popularize astrology via the horoscopes they began to publish, setting the Sun's dates at the beginning and end of each sign of the Zodiac, and making astrological predictions for each of the Sun signs.

This was later refined by relating the Sun-sign astrology to the yearly movements of the planets, but even so, considering that in Britain there is a population of well over 60 million people and there are but twelve sun signs, each newspaper horoscope covers 5.5 million Britons!

# The elements

The four elements – Fire, Earth, Air and Water – play their part in astrology, three Zodiac signs each sharing the nature of one or other of them.

Fire is associated with the creative, with vitality, enthusiasm, excitement, passion, energy, exhibitionism and having the ability to entertain.

Earth is the material element, concerned as it is with routine, the law, savings, tradition, building and legacy.

Air is the element of the intellect, of ideas, the thought process, explanations, gregariousness and discussion.

Water is all about the emotions – about love and anger, sentiment and sympathy, caring and tenderness.

# The signs

## Aries, the ram
## (21 March – 20 April)

*Mars, Fire*

With Fire its element and Mars its ruler, people born under Aries are often lean and muscular, muddy complexioned and red-haired.

They are the first to welcome a stranger with a warm handshake and a warmer smile. They are completely extrovert and will initiate adventures at the drop of a hat, regardless of danger. Busy, restless, impatient, they are enthusiastic about new ventures – at the beginning at least. Having probably done the spadework to get them off the ground, they soon get bored and are keen to move on to pastures new at the first opportunity. But then, their enthusiasm will have inspired others to take over.

That's the good news! The worst in them comes out when they are involved in an argument (which they probably started): if they have something to say, out it comes, regardless of whom they hurt. They are quick-tempered and if they have ever heard the word 'diplomacy' it's doubtful if they ever bothered to find out what it means!

If they are ever tempted to tell a lie, they needn't bother, for they can't! But if you told them that, they wouldn't believe you, for no one, but no one, can do anything better than an Aries, no matter what. They are always right and quick to blame others when things go wrong. They loathe anyone interfering in their affairs, even if most of the decisions they make are on impulse.

They love to be the centre of attraction, are first on the dance floor at a party – and first back in their seat. And tell an Arian a story in company and it will instantly be capped by a better one.

But, they make good, if slightly authoritarian bosses. Career-wise, they are attracted to sport, politics and the armed services. If they are going to be off work, it will probably be with a headache or, later in life, with ear troubles.

Arians have a strong romantic streak and like nothing better than being flattered and appreciated. They are quick to give their heart – and just as quick to offer it to another . . . and another . . . and another. If any sign is likely to change his or her mind at the altar, it's an Arian, but if they do say, I do!' they will expect that there will be one set of rules for them and another, more restrictive one for their spouse!

In matters of the heart, their most compatible signs are Leo and Sagittarius. The former has a similar outlook in life to Arians, and like them know exactly what they want and how to get it. The two signs are freedom-loving and adventurous and have an immediate understanding of one another. Sagittarians are suitable partners because they are usually prepared to try the new and unusual to keep their Arian partner happy.

People born under Aries are often attracted to Aquarians, but those born under the sign of the water carrier are independent and unwilling to allow themselves to be stifled by overpowering Aries. Marriage between the two? No! A passionate, mutually enjoyable affair. Perhaps!

And if a secretive, sexy Scorpio shimmies into an Arian's life, sparks will fly! There was a time when both these signs were ruled by Mars, the god of war, and war is the likely outcome of a liaison between the two.

## Taurus, the bull (21 April – 21 May)

*Venus, Earth*

Ruled by Venus and influenced by Earth, people with Taurus as their Sun sign are often very physically attractive with large eyes and a fine complexion, and shiny hair that often flops Hugh-Grant style over their forehead. They are affectionate and charming (sometimes a bit too charming to appear sincere), and like Coleridge's Ancient Mariner can hypnotize whoever they talk to with their glittering eyes and steady, innocent gaze.

Taureans are instinctive creatures and often come to major decisions without really knowing how they reached them. And hence their talent for making amazing blunders. They don't give their trust easily, though, and it's unwise to meddle in a Taurean's affairs without being asked to do so.

Other signs are often duped into believing that patience is one of the Taurean's virtues. Wrong! Dig a little deeper and you'll find they are as stubborn as the proverbial mule. Not the most imaginative creatures, they won't be rushed into things, disliking risks and gambles. And whereas other signs may be happy with wool, whisky and Welsh rarebit, it's cashmere, champagne and caviar for luxury-loving Taureans. Their love of money often draws Taureans to choose banking as a career; their need for security may encourage them to look to the civil service. When they fall in love, Taureans are very possessive. Ideally, they need a conscientious and ambitious partner who will work towards their mutual goals in a methodical manner. Capricorn and Virgo are the signs the Taurean should look to, sharing with him or her a need for security while at the same time valuing their independence. Cancerians would also make good life partners, were it not for their often crabby, moody nature. Scorpios should also be avoided by the Taurean who is looking for love, for both signs can be over-possessive and matching one with the other can be disastrous. It's this trait that causes Taureans to shy away from forming deep, emotional relationships until they have gained a fair bit of experience in matters of the heart – that's why Taureans are often last in a circle of friends to walk down the aisle. They will wait, and wait, and wait and when the right person comes along they know instinctively that that's the one. And when that happens and the knot is tied, they will expect total fidelity and security, both emotional and financial, for the married Taurean's home is a luxurious nest to which friends will always be welcomed and lavishly entertained.

## Gemini, the twins (22 May – 21 June)

*Mercury, Air*
Geminis are eternally youthful, never seeming to surrender to the ravages of time, unlike the rest of us. Bright eyed, friendly and smiling, they dazzle strangers and friends

alike into agreeing to anything they want. Immaculate in appearance, they work at keeping themselves in tip-top shape: although there are twelve signs in the Zodiac, it's a better than twelve-to-one chance that the person pounding the treadmill next to you at the gym is a Gemini.

They are never wrong. Not because they are always right, but because, with Mercury as their planet, they are mercurial of mind, forever changing it to make it hard for anyone to pin them down and prove them incorrect. They are curious to the extreme. If anyone tells them half a secret, they will get to the bottom of the rest of it, by hook or by crook. They love a good argument and have the annoying knack of finding the flaw in the opposition's case and destroying it with one quick remark. They love words, big and small, especially the big ones no one else understands, and use them superbly – in or out of context.

With air their element, it's no surprise that Geminis are constantly on the move. They hate being stuck in the same place for too long, be it in a long meeting or even in the same house. Their minds are on the go twenty-four hours a day and they are never content to limit themselves to do one thing at a time. Someone once said that if you want something done, ask a busy woman: if she's a Gemini, all the better.

Being romantically involved with a Gemini is an exciting, stimulating affair – not necessarily a long-term attachment, but a breathtaking one all the same. They are best suited to Librans and Aquarians – fellow air signs. Aquarians share with them a need for freedom; Librans love peace at all costs, so will be more than happy to put up with Gemini's faults, and their shared love of beauty will give them many common interests. Geminis are often attracted to Leos, but the lion of the Zodiac will usually prove too much for restless Gemini. If there is one sign that Geminis should steer clear of at all costs, it's Capricorn, a sign with many virtues, most of which bore Gemini to distraction.

But whichever signs lands Gemini for a partner, it should take heed that the heavenly twins seem to be quicker to the divorce courts than other signs – so it's no surprise that many of the most – divorced celebrities have Gemini as their Sun sign. For freedom is always vital to Gemini and whoever sets their sights at one or other of them should remember this before moving in for the marital kill. But, with their love of words, oh how they can set the heart a-flutter: get a love letter from a Gemini and treasure it. Not because it's rare, but because the words will sing off the page and penetrate even the hardest heart. And it may be a tad cynical to say it, but there are times when love is not the reason for a Gemini to walk down the aisle. Security? Perhaps. Or a step up the social ladder? Maybe. But love that's destined to last forever...?

Career-wise, broadcasting, journalism or a literary career is ideal for word-loving Geminis. They need to communicate and they can. They also feel that they can break free whenever they want – so it's no surprise to learn that many freelance workers or those who prefer temporary work to plodding along the career path, are born under the sign of Gemini.

## Cancer, the crab (22 June – 23 July)

### The Moon, Water

It may seem unkind to say so, but if you know someone who doesn't seem to be in the right proportions –

be they tall and thin, or short and dumpy – it's likely that you know a Cancerian! With their crab-like long arms and slender legs, they seem to glide along, almost as if they are afraid to take their feet off the ground in case they fall over.

You might also recognize them by their clothes. Whereas 'mix and match' is a maxim that fashion writers often advocate, 'mix and clash' is Cancer's maxim. And not only do their clothes not match, but the enthusiastic way in which they tuck in at table, can sometimes result in the odd food stain that 'nothing will budge' appearing on blouse, shirt or tie.

Cancer is ruled by the Moon, so it's hardly surprising that the crabs of the Zodiac are changeable, over-emotional and sensitive. But, on the other hand, they can surprise by being the strong, silent type who hates arguments and will do anything to avoid them, and will remain calm in the most difficult situations. And although no one knows who penned the phrase, 'revenge is a dish best eaten cold,' chances are it was a Cancerian. Slight or offend a Cancerian and they don't go seeking immediate revenge – they wait for weeks, months, even years and then strike when the iron is cool. But every bad side has a good one, and if you do a Cancerian a favour, they will never forget it and you have a friend who will stand by you for life.

Although they may not seem so, they are sensitive souls and what may have been intended as a jokey criticism may well go deep – while smiling on the outside, they may be sobbing their hearts out on the inside. They are good at giving the impression they think is expected of them. If you're talking to one and they are not the least bit interested in the subject, they will nod wisely, smile at the right moment and sigh when they feel that's what you expect – but what you are saying is going in one ear and out the other! But if you are talking about something that interests them, they can store information and organize it as efficiently as a computer.

Other signs often find Cancer difficult to make out and, because they often have dual natures, what one person sees as a charming, vivacious, sympathetic soul, another will see as a moody, uncompromising b******. If they like you, you will be first to know for they will go out of their way to be friendly, but if they take a scunner (a lovely Scottish word for dislike) to you, they won't even bother to give you the time of day. They'll look through you, talk over you: you're simply not there as far as they are concerned!

They like their privacy and the phrase, 'his home is his castle', could have been invented for them. They use their strong imaginations to dream up all sorts of fantasies, especially sexual ones – but do little to put them into practice. And if their lover is unfaithful, that's the one time they act out of character and seek immediate revenge. Although they share certain traits with Scorpios and Pisceans, these two signs offer rich hunting grounds for the Cancerian in search of a mate (especially if the male in the relationship is the Scorpio). They are often attracted to Libras but find them a bit too fickle after a while. They regard Virgos as potential friends rather than potential mates. And Sagittarians? Too versatile and too willing to seek their pleasures away from the home and family for Cancer's liking.

When it comes to choosing a career, they are often tempted to go into catering for their love of food makes them creative chefs. And being sympathetic souls, they often look to medicine or social work for job opportunities.

# Leo, the lion (24 July – 23 August)

*The Sun, Fire*

If any of the signs associated with mythological animals look like the eponymous beast, it's Leo. Slender and athletic of body, and with a fine mane of (often wild) hair, Leos look like lions. Remember those ads that showed a seven-stone weakling having sand kicked in his face by a muscular Adonis? Chances are it was a Leo who was kicking up the sandstorm! And the female of the species shares these exhibitionist tendencies with her male.

All Leos love to be the centre of attention and thrive on admiration. They thrive on challenges and if they say they will do something they will do it with the energy, enthusiasm and vitality that their element, Fire, sparks in them.

The word 'failure' does not come into their vocabulary, and their self-confidence can inspire some or make others loathe them. They set their goals and achieve them through their enthusiastic determination.

They can be so open that some people think them naïve, but they love impressing people and if they get the scent of envy in their nostrils they love it. They don't set out to offend people, but if they do and they realize they have been offensive, they won't apologize: attack is the best form of Leo's defence. An asked-for apology will be met with such subtle insults that whoever feels offended will often end up doing the apologizing, mumbling, 'Sorry, I didn't understand what you were getting at,' and slinking off before they see the smirk of triumph on Leo's face. And woe betide anyone who interrupts a Leo when he's eating.

Like their feline counterparts, when food is in their sights, nothing else matters. They make fabulous hosts, though – and if you aren't suitably and obviously impressed, don't expect to be asked back.

Aries and Sagittarius are the two signs under which Leo is likely to find his soulmate. Arians, like Leos, stimulate each other and though there may be tremendous battles of will between the two, as they both want to be first in everything that they do, they will both enjoy the other's company. Sagittarians are the ones that Leo trusts above all other signs, and finds them the most physically attractive. Geminis and Leos are often attracted to each other, but as Leo likes to be boss, the flames of passion are soon doused. The Lion and the Scorpion may also enjoy a brief fling, but Scorpio's tendency to exercise too much authority soon rankles with Leo. But when the affair is over, there usually remain the bonds of strong friendship. The one sign that Leos should avoid at all cost is Virgo – far too nit-picking and critical for a sign that loathes being criticised.

Whoever Leo decides to settle down with, usually after a great deal of contemplation, must always be one hundred per cent loyal. They must be willing to be subservient on occasions and also to tolerate their partner flirting, often outrageously, in their presence if they are feeling in need of admiring attention.

In selecting a career, Leo usually decides on one that gives him the chance to show off – so it's no surprise that the stage attracts them like magnets, and Leo actors, with their vitality, enthusiasm, passion and energy, are the ones that are least likely to be resting, darling!

VIRGO

# Virgo, the virgin
# (24 August – 23 September)

*Mercury, Earth*

Virgo's element is Mercury, the Messenger of the Gods who was forever darting hither and thither. It's no surprise then that those born under the sign of the Virgin have fascinating eyes that seem to be everywhere at once, trying to take in everything at once. And they can change their facial expressions at the drop of a hat: a sympathetic smile for someone who needs comforting one moment, a wide grin for someone they're sharing a joke with the next. That's Virgo.

With Earth as their element, it's no surprise that they love routine and cleanliness, law and order. They are forever scrubbing and washing and are so neat and tidy, often dressed in their hallmark grey or blue, they could have stepped straight from a clothes-shop window.

They tend to be the most critical sign of the Zodiac, ever ready to have a go at others and being the first to point out their mistakes (which they never make themselves). Given the chance, they will organize things down to the last detail and are first to take the credit for the work others have done at their behest. However, when the need arises, they will work harder than anyone else to make sure that a schedule is kept to and a job done the best it can be.

Their darting eyes are first to pick out a flaw in others, no matter how small, and the quick wit and use of double entendre they have at their command, enables them to point these flaws out in a way that makes those unfortunate enough to be at the receiving end believe that Virgo knows every skeleton in the cupboard.

Curiously, despite their ability to discomfort people, Virgos need interesting friends around them all the time – and they're not afraid to use them to increase their store of knowledge and to up their bank balance. But don't even think about exploiting a Virgo – they will cast their eye over their wide circle of friends and select the one who can best help them get their own back.

When it comes to matters of the heart, Virgos are as pernickety in choosing a partner as they are in every other aspect of their lives. Their ideal partners will have class and cash – in marriage, love is an added bonus for the virgins of the Zodiac. Once they have tied the knot they will try to carry on with the busy social lives they enjoyed in their bachelor days, showing to their trophy partners just how lucky they are to have landed a popular, sociable Virgo.

With a deep-rooted need for security, Virgo is well matched with Capricorn, a sign that complements the Virgin and will strive to achieve their mutual goals. They will massage each other's egos – but whether they do so with even an ounce of sincerity is questionable. Virgos share a love of beauty with Taureans who will make suitable marriage partners. Not Geminis or Sagittarians though: Virgos may well dally with one or other of them for a while, but in the long term, although they may build a lasting friendship, Virgo will not trust either sign one hundred per cent. Scorpios are a bit too deep and secretive for Virgos and as for those born under Aries – the two signs should steer clear of each other in the romantic stakes for match critical Virgo with fiery Aries and the sparks will not just fly, they will explode!

Virgos are so well organized, they make excellent secretaries – knowing exactly where everything is and having an instinct of knowing when it will be needed. But with their tendency to take over, many bosses find themselves regretting the day they hired Mr or Ms Perfect! And if you are a moment of two late for an appointment be it a business or hospital one and the receptionist slaps your fingers for your tardiness – it's even money that he or she is a Virgo!

## Libra, the scales (24 September – 23 October)

*Venus, Air*

With Venus as the sign's ruling planet, it's hardly surprising that Librans are the most beautiful of all the signs in the Zodiac. A graceful, elegant frame, a creamy, clear complexion, glowing, velvety hair, fine bone structure and teeth that could feature in a toothpaste commercial. If they have an Achilles heel, it is (appropriately enough) their feet which are often unusually large: but such are their other attributes that no one notices.

Flirtatious by nature, they have few scruples in using their good looks to help them get what they want. They thrive on love and attention, have perfect manners, are generous (if a teensy bit over-sophisticated) hosts to friend and stranger alike and, because they hate arguments will do anything to avoid one, or if it's too late, will be first to pour oil on troubled waters. That's hardly surprising, given that their Zodiac sign is the scales. But what is surprising is that they often tend to go to extremes. A glass of house champagne? Make it a bottle of the best Bollinger. A rug to put on the gleaming, wooden floor that stretches as far as the eye can see? Make it a silk kilim!

Surprisingly, in matters of the heart, Librans often need to be coaxed out of their shell before they will declare themselves, and versatile, independent Gemini is just the sign to do this, helping Libra to achieve the balance that is so important in his or her life. Aquarians share with Libra a tendency to call a spade a spade and a dislike or anything false or imitative, and the two signs can be well matched romantically. The Taurean tendency to be possessive mars what could otherwise be a reasonable pairing, but the two make good, long-term friends. Scorpio's sharp-tongue jars with Libra and the two should steer well clear of one another.

Being turned down by whoever it is they fall for is something that cuts Librans to the quick. They simply can't understand how anyone could do that to them and will eventually convince themselves that the other person obviously didn't realize what they've turned down, poor things! And when an affair breaks up, so strong is the Libran fear of loneliness that they plunge into another one at the first opportunity.

With air as Libra's element and socializing one of the words associated with it, it should come as no surprise to whomsoever a Libran plights his or her troth that life seems to be one long party – for they love throwing them and any excuse will do.

Other words linked to the element air are ideas, thought and explanation. That could explain why so many Librans are fascinated by politics and may well take it up as a career. Design is also a field that attracts them, but they should steer clear of banking or any job in the financial sector. Money matters and Libra simply don't go together!

# Scorpio, the scorpion
# (24 October – 22 November)

*Pluto, Water*

'Hypnotic' and 'Magnetic' are two words that are often applied to Scorpios. The first thing you notice about a typical Scorpio is not his or her complexion, which is often sallow, and it's not his or her hair, even though it can be so uncontrollable that it looks as if it hasn't seen a comb for weeks. Their height? Just average. Their build? Just average. But their eyes! They don't so much look at you: they look right through you.

Their superficial manner disguises a volcanic temper that will erupt the moment anyone steps out of line. They have a memory like a computer – names, places, events, phone numbers (when a Scorpio uses a phone number chances are he will never have to look it up again – it's committed to memory forever). When a Scorpio listens to what seems to be trivial gossip, he may look as if he's paying no more attention than anyone else. But his analytical mind is taking in everything and when the time comes, tiny facts that everyone else has long forgotten will come out, honed and weapon-sharp – often in the devastating retort for which Scorpios are famous.

With Pluto, the planet that reveals our ability to effect transformation, as its ruling body, it's no surprise to learn that Scorpios can change at the drop of a hat – polite and charming one minute, rude and aggressive the next. They're never happier than when they are proving someone wrong – something they can do with alarming speed and horrible accuracy: no wonder that Scorpios make excellent detectives – they'll spot the flaw in a story right away.

When Scorpios give their friendship, it's for life. They

tend to overlook their friends' faults apart from one: disloyalty. If a Scorpio finds out that a friend has been disloyal that's it. He will never forget and never forgive, for when a Scorpio says, 'I'm never going to speak to you again,' he means it – no matter at what cost to himself. And that's typical Scorpio, if he wounds himself in the process of hitting out at someone else, that's just too bad.

When Scorpios find that a friend is ill, it brings out everything that's good about them, for then they become astonishingly sympathetic and helpful – and there's nothing they won't do to help, no matter how much it puts them out.

They are the most passionate and overtly sexual sign of the Zodiac, lustful lovers who like to get as good as they give, then some more. But, they do have a tendency to overestimate their prowess in the bedroom. Their desire to dominate makes Scorpios an ideal match for Cancerians who often like to take the back seat in a relationship. They are also well paired with Pisceans, one of whose traits is an inability to make decisions, something Scorpios adore. The scorpion and the lion get on well, but are best advised to stay friends rather than lovers. Scorpio and Capricorn share a tendency to keep secrets from their partners and when the cat gets out of the bag, claws are unsheathed and the fur flies in all directions. As Scorpios have to be the dominant partner in a relationship, anyone born under the sign who finds themselves attracted to one of the same should think twice, three times, before taking matters any further.

In selecting a career, Scorpios love the challenges of big business and jobs in which their negotiating skills can be best used. But no matter what career path they choose Scorpios, as one well-known astrologer wittily observed, like to start at the top and work their way up.

SAGITTARIUS

# Sagittarius, the archer (23 November – 21 December)

*Jupiter, Fire*

If one or two of your friends are taller and more athletic than the others, the chances are that they were born under the sign of the archer – Sagittarius. They always seem to be on the move, which might explain why very few Sagittarians are fat!

Fire is Sagittarius's element, and, with one of the words associated with that element being excitement, it should come as no surprise that to many of them life is an exciting game, full of gambles and opportunities that should be grabbed at every turn. And with the typical Sagittarian's luck, the gamble is likely to pay handsome dividends and the chances taken lead to an ever increasing progression of opportunities.

They are charming, something they are happy to use to get them out of any trouble their happy-go-lucky, extrovert natures may land them in, and people will forgive them anything, which may explain the Sagittarian tendency to see life through rose-coloured glasses. Voltaire didn't specify under which sign Dr Pangloss in the novella *Candide* was born, but with his watchword being, 'It's all for the best in the best of all possible worlds,' he must have been a Sagittarius.

Similarly, J. M. Barrie never tells us what Peter Pan's Sun sign is. With the Sagittarian desire to stay young forever (and they will spend a fortune on lotions and potions as well as diet plans and exercise regimes to help them to do so) it's safe to say that Peter was born under the sign.

Expansive Jupiter is the sign of the archer's ruling planet, and one linked with excess. Maybe that's why Sagittarians can fall in love at first sight, and can be in love with more than one person at the same time. A new conquest is a great morale booster to a Sagittarian, and they are always on the lookout for someone new to dazzle with their open-handed, open-hearted personalities.

The Sagittarian love of independence makes it hard for those who set their hearts on marrying one to march their catch up the aisle. And whoever does land one, must be prepared to hide their jealousy when their spouse announces that they are off to meet an old flame to talk over times past.

Leo and Sagittarius go well with each other, the lion having the knack of keeping the archer on the right track and stopping them making fools of themselves at parties, something their extrovert nature encourages. They are also good in bed together. Fellow fire sign Aries is also a good match for Sagittarius as long as the ram understands that the archer is not expected to surrender completely to it. Gemini and Sagittarius are often too alike to make it safe to take the marital plunge; Taurus is far too possessive to allow Sagittarians the looseness of rein they need, and Scorpio's secretiveness and deviousness will drive open-, broad-minded Sagittarius to distraction.

Sagittarians are often the intellectuals of the Zodiac and no matter what career they choose, it must be one that allows them freedom of expression. And being imaginative, they can make good lawyers – and even better writers.

CAPRICORN

# Capricorn, the goat (22 December – 20 January)

*Saturn, Earth*

Sometimes small in stature, and with dark, piercing eyes, Capricorns often give the impression that they think whoever talks to them is only doing so for their own motives. That's why they often find it hard to smile, but when they do . . . it's like watching the Sun break through a stormy sky, turning the world gold.

Earth is their element, one associated with routine and tradition. And that's Capricorn – plodding along, sticking to plans, but getting there – always getting there – in the end. If there were twelve cardinal virtues and each one was ascribed to a planet, then Capricorn's would surely be Patience.

They may not give their friendship easily for they seem to have a self-imposed barrier around them. But when they let it slip and invite someone through, the force of warmth of their personalities can be as overpowering as it is unexpected.

Capricorns often suffer from low self-esteem, but they don't hold anyone else in high regard either, so it doesn't make much difference to them. If there's an injustice to be handed out, Capricorn will be first in the queue, hands outstretched to take it. But, when they think they have been treated really unfairly, they will bide their time, waiting for the right moment to get revenge (although if you accused them of this, they would look at you in open-mouthed disbelief).

Capricorns are a bit of a cold fish in the romantic department. Not for them a long, sweet seduction. Not for them hours of world-moving foreplay. With

Capricorn, it's 'what you see is what you get and let's get it over with as quickly as possible, I've got better things to do'.

Marriage to a Capricorn is marriage for life. Their steadfastness and loyalty are legend, and they expect the same in return. Virgos make good marriage partners – they will help their spouses run their business affairs efficiently and keep them in line in the domestic front. Taurus often offers what Capricorn is looking for in love. But if a Capricorn is considering a Gemini for the marriage bed, best think again: Gemini lacks the ambition that Capricorn needs to achieve complete fulfilment. Aquarians are too independent and eccentric to make a good match with Capricorn.

But if one sign should be married, it's Capricorn. Marriage is often the making of a Capricorn. It brings them out of their shell and helps them to see beyond their self-imposed horizons.

Capricorns, with the methodical, well-planned approach to things make good businessmen. They also make good teachers, lawyers and politicians. They are good at using the latest IT to help them achieve their goals, and as they have little respect for authority, when they do achieve them, it is through their own efforts rather than using the favour of others to help them on to the top rung.

# Aquarius, the water bearer (21 January – 19 February)

*Uranus, Air*
Tall, with a high forehead, the typical Aquarian often has excellent bone structure and, with Uranus the planet of the unconventional as ruler

of the sign, he or she often sports an unusual hair style and fashionable, sometimes ultra-fashionable, clothes.

They are frank, with an open attitude to life, and although they like to create a good impression on those they meet, if they don't they will shrug their shoulders and carry on regardless. Independent of mind, they often seem to take two, three times longer than anyone else to do things: not because they are slow-witted but because they are so independent that the thought of asking anyone else for help is foreign to their nature.

They tend to take a universal view of things, preferring to take an interest in mankind as a whole rather than in the individual in particular. But, that said, point Aquarius to an underdog and they will champion it; show them a lost cause and they will fight it.

Their eccentric behaviour often finds them the centre of gossip. Aquarians don't mind: they are probably well aware that there is an element of truth about it. But if anyone goes too far with an Aquarian they will find themselves on the receiving end of one of the most incisive and cruel wits in the Zodiac. One razor-sharp quip will cut the offender to the bone, leaving him in awe at the speed with which the remark was made, while at the same time admiring the skill with which the words were phrased.

Associated with the element air, which is connected with ideas, thoughts and explanations, it should be no surprise that Aquarians are very intellectual, seeking to expand their knowledge of just about everything and anything at every opportunity.

Anyone who falls in love with one of the water-bearers has their hands full. Give them the slightest excuse to be bored and they are off – riding into the sunset with a new lover in tow. That said, while the affair is proceeding, Aquarius is the most loyal of lovers: it's just that give one even half a chance to get bored and that's it. In a flash the eye will wander and it's all over.

Libra and Gemini are the signs that are ideally suited to Aquarius – they have many common interests, share a love of freedom and will pull out all the stops to keep romance alive, especially in the bedroom. They also share an intellectual streak and will have no difficulties in communicating with each other. Aquarians often find themselves attracted to Leos and Sagittarians, but after a time, the lion and the archer will start to get on the water-carrier's nerves. Cancerians are too much the loner for Aquarians, and romantic liaisons between the two should be avoided.

Aquarians often look to science as a career, particularly astronomy and radiography. They also make good actors and writers.

# Pisces, the fish (20 February – 20 March)

*Neptune, Water*
Whereas some signs bless or curse those born under them with a typical appearance, Pisceans come in all shapes and sizes – although many of them will confess that they are just a little over the weight they would like to be. Being a water sign and with Neptune as their guiding planet, it should be no surprise to learn that those born under the sign often have eyes that shine like deep emerald pools.

Pisceans rely on first impressions. Dazzle one on first meeting with ready wit and a quick quip or two and they will assume you are the Justin Bieber of your generation.

Appear down and depressed and they will firmly believe that you are an eternal streak of misery.

They have the happy knack of encouraging people to come to their aid whenever they need it. They rarely need to ask for directions if they are lost. They will simply stand there looking just a little helpless and someone is almost guaranteed to come and say, 'Can I help you?'

Neptune, the sign's ruling planet, blurs reality and fantasy, so it's no surprise that Pisceans are the daydreamers of the Zodiac. If there's a problem, that's for one of the other signs to solve. And try to get one to make a decision? Drawing hen's teeth is easier. Neptune also tells us of our deep-felt need to feel at one with others. This makes Pisceans especially happy people – laughing and smiling more than most other signs, especially when they are trying to impress the opposite sex. They hate being alone and really need their friends to give them the affection they crave twenty-four hours a day.

They can be highly strung and prone to extravagant displays of emotion and temper. Rudolf Nureyev, the famous Russian dancer, was typically Piscean in this respect. It was not unknown for him to pick up a heavy ashtray in a fit of temper and smash it through a rehearsal room floor-to-ceiling mirror, and then to charm everyone with his extravagant display of apology even before the last shard had fallen to the floor.

They often give the impression that they have no idea what they want out of life, and in this case, impressions run deep. But no matter. Given Pisces' luck something will surely turn up, and chances are that someone else will have made it happen.

They are forever on the move – and pinning one down is almost an impossibility. If you have Piscean friends, you'll see a lot of them over a short period, and then they vanish for months on end. Ask where they have been and they look at you with that typical wide-eyed innocence, shrug their shoulders and say, 'What do you mean?'

When they fall in love, their partner has to learn to treat them with kid gloves. They don't mind being dominated, as long as they can see the fairness of it. They are often heard to tell their partners that they (the partner) are too good for them. Agree and they will be hurt to the quick. And remember that they need to be fussed over: if they're not they will think that there is something wrong – not with them, but with you.

Cancerians, with their matchless ability to 'understand' are the ideal match for Pisceans, and Scorpio does very well too, being able to help Pisces make important decisions that she could never reach on her own. An attraction to Gemini is best kept to an affair that both will enjoy, rather than anything longer lasting. Virgos' fussiness and critical eye can wound Pisces, but the two signs can go with the flow of friendship. And Aries is far too bossy and on the go all the time for Pisces ever to settle down with.

With their dislike of responsibility, Pisceans don't make the best bosses in the world. But they make excellent carers, and so many of them find nursing an attractive proposition. And with a deep-rooted love of animals, they make excellent vets.